You Are Born to Lead

You Are Born to Lead

REFLECT, ADAPT, AND MAKE AN IMPACT RIGHT NOW

Christine McLaren and Kelly McCleary

Born to Lead Press

ISBN: 0692923861
ISBN 13: 9780692923863

Acknowledgments

Christine's Acknowledgments

'd like to offer a special thank-you to my husband, Chris, whose patience with this project spanned years, countless hours (including on a couple of vacations when I had no other time for editing), and a few pep talks when the reality and complexity of writing a book set in. He also provided very detailed, thoughtful feedback on the book that helped make it something Kelly and I believe will truly help our readers. I'm also so thankful for my wonderful twin daughters, who never doubted for a second that we would finish and who cheered me on throughout the process. Their gentle hearts and wisdom inspire me every day.

Kelly is one of my favorite former clients and someone I truly enjoyed working with—both on the leadership team we were on and while writing this book together. I'm most thankful for the e-mail she sent to me while I was deep in the woods camping in Ely, Minnesota, one summer with family, which read, "I've been reading your blog, and it sounds very similar to what I've been thinking about lately. Would you be interested in writing a book together?" Write a book? It was a lifelong dream. And yet, it was still just an item on the bucket list that might have never happened had she not shown the interest in my perspective and sparked the idea that became a reality. She also stuck through this book's completion despite life challenges that would have overcome anyone else I know. Kelly's patience, courage, persistence, and resilience probably deserved their own chapters in the book.

All my past business customers, leaders, managers, HR peers, and supervisors deserve a big thank-you as well. I learned so much over the years watching and working with all of you through some pretty big organizational challenges.

Thank you to all the countless individuals I've spoken to throughout the last few years regarding this book. You offered unique perspectives, firsthand experience, support, advice, and encouragement that helped in little ways leading to this final product. I apologize for not being able to include everybody here.

Most of all, thank you to our readers. To know there are people out there who care as much as we do about this topic, who want to make an impact in and out of the workplace, is our "why."

Kelly's Acknowledgments

I owe a debt of gratitude to the leaders I've worked with who've shown me how to lead others to engagement. You showed me that effective leadership is shockingly simple: making others feel valued. I'm grateful that you took me under your wing, that you saw a glimmer of something in me when I was still raw and rough and clumsy as a leader. I'm especially grateful for those of you with the courage and the caring to give me the direct and candid feedback that I needed, for holding a mirror up to me when I couldn't even see my hand in front of my face.

A special thank-you to Cindy Tade for being my best friend for the last twenty-five years and for giving your wisdom and the candid feedback necessary to make this book better. Thank you to Eric Sanders, a leader whose career I have been cheerfully watching since being transferred to his team. You gave generously of your busy schedule to provide good input into this effort; I look forward to continuing to follow your leadership success. Thank you to Barry Mongan, who wasn't here for this go-around but whose wise and thoughtful feedback from the last time guided me once again.

There is no thank-you big enough for my coauthor, Christine. She followed me on this leap of faith into the unknown, showing infinite patience when life events interrupted the writing of this book. As she has done since I met her, she made both the book and me far better than I would have been on my own.

Finally, a thank-you to my family. My amazing children teach me something every day—this is a true gift, since all leaders must continuously learn. As with every other accomplishment in my life, I couldn't have possibly done it without the support and encouragement of my husband, Russ. You've always wanted me to be all I could be. The irony is that was never possible without you.

Table of Contents

Introduction

*There are all kinds of ways to learn to be
a leader. The foolish way is to think that
there is a type of ideal leader, and try
to become that. The smart way is to…
find out where and how you can become
effective in making changes in the world.*

—Bruce L. Payne

Why This Book Is Different

After decades of trial and error, feel-good leadership development courses, great and dismal bosses, and many (many) mistakes, we've written the book we wish we'd had earlier in our careers as leaders. We want to change the dynamic, empowering you with the tools you need to take charge of your own leadership development and helping you develop the very best and most important leadership tool: your unique self. We believe that being prepared in advance for each new experience on your leadership journey can help you become more successful, more quickly, and can limit the impact of the mistakes you may make along the way.

We feel uniquely qualified to take up this cause. While many people who write books on leadership development are academics who haven't walked in their readers' shoes, we are our own target audience. We've learned some tough lessons during our combined sixty years of leadership experience, but we've also been successful. We've walked, stumbled, and sprinted on the "trial and error" path to leadership, as leaders of teams and with the many leaders and employees we've coached. We've taken great risks, with significant career and life changes. With these collective perspectives, we've gained the unique ability to make the overcomplicated and overresearched topic of leadership development approachable and effective for all. This is our passion. It can be better. Together, by helping leaders and employees become their best selves, achieve more of their goals, and gain more career satisfaction, we can help create high-performing, innovative organizations that don't need engagement surveys to tell them whether their employees are engaged.

First, it's important to define what a leader is. A leader is, simply, someone others follow. Even if you don't directly manage others, you can still be a leader, influencing others around you to follow your lead. Whether we lead a large team or are individual contributors in a technical or professional role, most of us want to be leaders: to make a positive difference on those around us and on the organizations we serve. The goal of this book is to not only demystify the complexities of managing teams, but also to help point us toward making that positive impact in our little corner of the world, even if we're indirect leaders.

Some people aspire to be leaders from the beginning of their careers and work hard to make that happen. Others have leadership thrust upon them suddenly, bringing with them whatever strengths and opportunities they already possess. Few of us are fully ready to lead when the time comes, inherently possessing all the skills we need to help us lead successfully. No one wants to be a mediocre leader, but the reality is that most of us are. Denial of this fact is rampant: 97 percent of leaders rate their ability to lead as at or above average,[1] statistically impossible given the definition of "average."

Without a clear consensus on how (and which) leaders become successful, it's understandable that many organizations struggle to choose and develop good leaders consistently. Countless leadership books and models unnecessarily complicate the task of developing leaders, and the "one size fits all" approach of most organizations toward leadership development often doesn't yield enough effective leaders. Some organizations develop robust but expensive programs, but then, because of the cost, limit them to senior executives or those considered high potential. These programs often do not reach the masses: the majority of the frontline supervisors who directly affect the engagement of their employees.

In theory, your boss should be a key resource in helping you meet your development needs. Unfortunately, bad bosses are the number-one reason people quit jobs.[2] Too many leaders have never had a good role model to help them develop, and, therefore, they may not have learned how to develop others. Many bosses were promoted because they were stars as individual contributors, not because they're good at developing other leaders.

At the time of this writing, there were almost two hundred thousand "leadership" books listed on Amazon; it's a topic widely studied and written about, and we'll refer to some of these references in our book. And yet, we see an unaddressed and widening gap of leadership in the workplace. While we can't fix all of the challenges that organizations face in properly selecting and equipping leaders, we *can* show you how to develop yourself, giving you a better chance at a purposeful career and at success. We can help you to better understand and express your unique gifts.

Our Vision and Promise

Our purpose for this book is to help you realize that to become a great leader, you don't need to try to become some*thing*, but to become some*one*. You'll perform best when you're acting authentically. With a simple, regular practice of self-awareness as shown in this book, you can adapt to any situation and confidently manage the increased complexity of more advanced roles as you progress in your career.

Formal leadership means only that you've been granted authority by your organization that encourages others to follow you, but many leaders gain followers without any formal authority. With thought and planning, you can be a leader from your first day on the job. Discovering how you uniquely lead from the very beginning will make it more likely that others at all levels will see you as the leader you want to be. Midcareer professionals or senior leaders have much to gain from our approach as well. We isolate the most important focus areas, which, in combination with your unique leadership self, will yield high-performing, successful teams.

We've designed this book to be a one-stop, lifelong resource no matter where you are in your career. By the end, you'll have a deep knowledge of yourself and will have applied that knowledge to a one-of-a-kind action plan that will help you lead right where you are today and into the future, based on your unique leadership capabilities and desires. You'll feel more in control, more purposeful, more grounded around your current circumstances, and—hopefully—more excited about your future.

CHAPTER 1

Our Book's Structure

*Nobody can go back and start a
new beginning, but anyone can start
today and make a new ending.*
—MARIA ROBINSON

"Advancing" your career today is less about being pro-moted or following a traditional career path than about managing increased complexity. Today, many leaders spend long periods of their career at the same level in a series of lateral moves, not just because there are fewer upward opportunities than in the past, but also because it's a means of strategically gaining a variety of leadership experiences. This makes practical sense: organizations, and the markets they serve, are growing more complex. We should expect leaders in these organizations to gain complex and diverse experiences to be most effective. Given this reality, we'll guide you through the discovery of how you uniquely lead. You can apply those lessons right now and into the future for increasing levels of complexity and responsibility.

Understanding the exact actions that will be most effective at each level—from individual contributor to the most senior positions—even before you reach them, gives you a chance to practice the new skills you'll need before the stakes get higher. Being ready for each step can help you keep from derailing during a step change, allowing your transitions to be learning opportunities instead of career-limiters.

Following are the four common leadership stages around which this book is organized. These stages are loosely progressive, in that they follow a traditional leadership path, starting with discovering your unique leadership self and working toward leading increasingly larger and more complex organizations. Although each transition provides some building blocks for the next, you may not experience them in a strictly linear way. You'll notice throughout these sections that, as complexity increases, focus decreases.

1) **Self-Leadership**

   Here's where you'll discover your unique leadership self. The self-awareness to look inward to assess and manage your values, inspiration, strengths, and opportunities, and to look outward to explore how you show up to others, is foundational to leading others and creating the right opportunities for yourself. The continuous practice of self-leadership is absolutely core to this entire book.

2) **Leading Others**

We'll explore the basic principles and skills for the most important job of any leader: to engage, motivate, and lead others toward accomplishing shared goals. This section explores the concepts of leadership and authority, how to build employee engagement, and how to coach and provide feedback.

3) **Leading Complexity**

This section covers the principles and skills necessary to manage larger, interdependent, and more complex teams, functions, and processes. Leading Complexity explores the advanced self-leadership concept of emotional intelligence, which has been correlated to effective leadership. It also covers how to influence others outside your sphere of authority, as well as how to engage larger teams where you don't have direct contact with all team members on a regular basis.

4) **Strategic Leadership**

Complex leadership concepts such as inspirational leadership, setting the tone, and change management may be encountered prior to senior leadership, but are generally required for success at that level. These skills are similar to those in Leading Others and Leading Complexity, but on a significantly larger scale. We also discuss other complex topics, such as leading global teams, challenges faced by women and minorities, and advice and tips for common career events, including layoffs and career changes.

Leadership Companion

We provide exercises at the end of each chapter to reinforce the two themes of self-assessment and adaptation. Leaders improve only when they develop a continuous cycle of self-reflection and then adjust to what that self-reflection teaches them. As you complete the exercises, they build on each other and begin to form a roadmap for your development as a leader. This roadmap will be more than a plan with valuable insights and actions for today; it will be your constant "Leadership Companion" for the future. Most of the worksheets are brief and will take only a few minutes to complete (the Knowing Yourself and Knowing Others exercises will take a bit longer). Building a true Leadership Companion to help you accomplish your goals is surprisingly easy—we'll outline the simple ways to do so. Our vision is that it's a living, breathing document that's always changing, reflecting each step on your path, helping you every step of the way.

The modest investment of time you'll need for completing these mini-assessments should yield you a return over the long run by helping you to avoid some of the most common leadership pitfalls and to build a more positive leadership brand. Think of this investment as replacing (or perhaps shortening) the time you would have spent stressing about whatever current challenge you're facing. We think you'll find it incredibly rewarding, because you're learning how *you* lead, not studying textbook material and doing theoretical assignments on how to fit into some model of leadership. You may have already mastered some of the topics in this book, while other challenges may not have presented themselves yet. Avoid the temptation to skip exercises simply because of where you are in your career, or if they feel a little familiar; ensuring that you've got the basics and getting refreshers at each level improves the likelihood that you'll be effective at every stage of your career.

We invite you to proceed through the Leadership Companion exercises in the way that works best for you. Some like to do them after each chapter while others prefer to wait until they've completed the book and can reflect for a bit before going back and doing them.

It's been enlightening to do these exercises ourselves and go back later to review them. Once they're completed, keep them with you, regularly review them, and allow them to serve as reminders of your unique leadership self. This practice helps you make the most of your current circumstances and improves the odds you'll find more reward from future decisions.

Finally, scalability is important to us, to benefit as many people as possible, so we've designed the Leadership Companion so that you can also take your team through the exercises, depending on your goals and the team's needs. This can serve two important functions: to build the growth and self-knowledge of individuals on the team; and, by doing the exercises together, to help build trust, break down barriers, and support the process of creating a high-performing team.

Let's get started building your brand, your voice, and your unique leadership self!

Leadership Companion Exercise: Getting Started

Assess

1. What do you hope to gain from reading this book?

    _____

    _____

    _____

2. What kind of leader do you want to be known as? List
    three to five words that illustrate how you want others
    to describe you.

    _____

    _____

    _____

3. What are your career goals at this time? These may be
    specific positions, achievements, experiences, learnings,
    service objectives, etc.

    _____

    _____

    _____

Adapt

4. What could you apply above to immediately make your job more appealing?

_____

_____

_____

Self-Leadership

SELF-LEADERSHIP: A PREVIEW

He who controls others is powerful, but he who has mastered himself is mightier still.
—LAO TZU

Self-management is perhaps the most underestimated characteristic of effective leadership, no matter what level you are. It's only reasonable that you should be able to demonstrate that you can manage yourself before being trusted to manage others. You need to be able to manage your own actions, as well as create positive interactions with those around you. Too much of leadership development is spent focusing outward: on leadership models, coaching tools, or the next job. An inward focus is more important to improving as a leader and is the first concept we'll explore.

Miscommunications and misunderstandings are common with any relationship, not just in the workplace. Bringing a strong understanding of your own beliefs, values, and triggers will make it easier to manage through those routine challenges.

Some common tools and frameworks can help you better manage your relationships at work. We'll explore these concepts in the next chapter.

CHAPTER 2

Knowing Yourself

*Sometimes, taking a job is like going
to a shrink or something, where you
get to know yourself better.*

—LEELEE SOBIESKI

Knowing Yourself Starts the True Path to Leadership

Many believe that the first step toward achieving their potential as a leader is figuring out what they want. That should be the last step.

Knowing yourself is the best place to start on your path to becoming a leader. It's difficult to lead effectively, point yourself in the right direction, or successfully adapt to changing circumstances until you've first done the hard work of understanding when you're at your best (and, equally importantly, when you're not). The ability to adapt isn't just how we improve as leaders;

rather, the ability to change as the environment changes will also represent a personal and professional advantage.

Adaptability and resilience are key ingredients for success in leaders, which is why we stress the importance of a regular cycle of self-assessment and adapting. There are also a couple of significant workplace trends driving the importance of being grounded in self-knowledge:

- Work teams are growing more diverse, both in terms of traditional definitions of diversity including ethnicity and gender, but also in terms of work practices, such as remote or project-based teams, which can contain people at a variety of levels and may change frequently.

- Economic and global uncertainty means your organization must be able to respond to change more quickly than ever, imposing a sense of urgency on its employees (you). That can mean drastic restructurings, process change, or worse: workforce reductions. You need to be ready with a plan to weather those changes. Entire industries and jobs are rapidly transforming. Stay up-to-date on those changes and respond with self-learning, or you could be at risk. Regularly spending time understanding and enhancing what sets you apart from others will help you maintain your competitive edge.

- Organizations increasingly expect an entrepreneurial mind-set at all levels of the organization, possibly using terms such as "adaptability" or "enterprising." Basically, they want employees who are proactive, who bring new ideas, and who can jump into a situation and make an immediate impact. Equally important is the ability to respond and lead people through change quickly. Knowing your values and strengths will help you plan ahead so that you know and can promptly communicate where you can best contribute. If you know yourself well, you can even be ahead of the curve, potentially inventing or suggesting new roles before they're needed.

- Finally, and probably the most straightforward and obvious reason for regular self-assessment: 70 percent of American workers are just plain miserable in their jobs.[3] That's millions of people trapped...living eight, ten, twelve hours a day unhappy and out of integrity with themselves. The only way out and forward is through simple but honest self-reflection over when to change and what to change to.

So, why don't many of us make the effort to really know ourselves? There are a number of reasons, including not knowing where to start, fear that you won't come up with anything unique, or not believing the effort is worthwhile. The question isn't whether these excuses are real, it's whether any of them are holding you back. If fear or not knowing where to start is the only thing between you and some regular time invested in understanding who you are and where you're going, remember that knowledge is power. There's no downside to investing the time in understanding yourself, except the time that you'll spend doing so. There are, however, very real potential downsides for *not* making this investment, including possibly limiting your effectiveness, your ability to adapt, or your ability to achieve your goals.

Knowing Yourself: A "How-To"

What does it really mean to "know yourself"? Many people would say that they understand themselves well, and that's largely true. But knowing yourself here means purposefully gathering specific data—both from you and from others—of which you may be only partially aware, in order to develop a plan that puts you in charge of your future, encourages adaptability, helps guide decisions, and empowers you to manage whatever comes your way. It's not about what you *do*, but, rather, who you *are*.

We propose a six-step process to knowing yourself. The tools in this section will provide meaningful information that can be directly applied and easily repeated for you to come back to in the future, to inform new opportunities or challenges. The goal of this section is to leave you with deep insights and a comprehensive picture into your true nature so that you can quickly assess your environment and adapt appropriately, assuredly choose a new path, or just feel at peace that you are where you're supposed to be right now.

The first of the six steps in knowing yourself is ensuring that you understand what inspires you, so you know how to get fulfillment from your job and develop the important leadership capability of inspiring others. A "Peak Moments" exercise can help you understand when you're truly inspired and at the top of your game; conversely, glancing back to times that truly challenged you and brought out your strongest emotions can help you identify and avoid the "blind spots" which can eventually catch up with you as career derailers. The next step is understanding your strengths. Knowing how you react to inevitable stress can also help you manage your performance as a leader. When you add the next two layers of self-knowledge—supplementing your self-assessment exercises with feedback from others and deciding how you want to serve—a clear picture will begin to emerge. Finally, these steps purposely build to the final step of discovering your core values. This is your voice: the impact you want to make, and your unique and valuable contribution. This is the foundation upon which you can successfully build your goals and dreams, and, ultimately, lead.

Step 1: What Inspires You?

Knowing what inspires you and having the discipline to remain inspired is an important aspect of achieving great things, engaging others, and being seen as a leader. People are perceptive, and they can absolutely tell the difference between an inspired leader and one who's only going through the motions. Inspiration creates energy and engagement. You might be wondering, "What's the difference between core values and inspiration?" They're similar, but you need both. Think of core values as what's important to you, while inspiration is what excites and motivates you. While living your core values in some way probably excites you, inspiration is taking your core values to the next level. For example, someone may have a core value of integrity, but if they think hard about what truly inspires them, it may be something that builds on that value; for example, innovating or seeing others grow and develop.

Tapping into your inspiration, particularly when you're not feeling inspired, doesn't have to be hard. A powerful way to gain accurate information about who you are and what inspires you is an exercise found in *Do More Great Work*, by Michael Bungay Stanier, which asks you to look back and answer the question, "What were your peak moments?"[4] The temptation is to describe ourselves by stating facts—education, work history, projects, and accomplishments. But facts are superficial and don't get at who you really are. This exercise rips away convention and asks you to describe peak moments when you felt you were at the top of your game—a high point in the job, a moment when you internally said "Yes!" Your peak moment connects you with that time when you felt most fulfilled, most stretched, most present, most yourself in your job. A peak moment is not necessarily a big accomplishment, but rather work in which you lost yourself...it is you, at your most authentic and best. The exercise is included at the end of this chapter. It doesn't take much time, and it should be interesting to see what surfaces for you.

Equally insightful is knowing your nonpeak moments: when you're at your worst, when you loathe what you're doing, when your head is there but your soul definitely is not. The goal of understanding nonpeak moments is only partially to try to avoid those situations in the future—it's often not that easy. Rather, knowing when we're not at our best can help us learn to cope effectively with irksome situations by understanding and better managing our emotional reactions. Including both in your Leadership Companion will be valuable in informing your goals in the next chapter.

Step 2: What Are Your Strengths?

Probably one of the top three interview questions of all time is "What are your strengths?" It is indeed important to know the answer, but the real magic in figuring out your strengths is in the ability to describe how to apply them. When you complete the peak moments exercise, you'll build on that information by asking yourself, "What strengths did I use in these peak moments?"

Tom Rath and Barry Conchie, in their book *Strengths Based Leadership*, made a compelling case for leaders to focus on strengths. Their argument is simple and backed by research: leaders who focus on employee strengths end up with higher employee engagement and better bottom lines.[5] Because your strengths will drive your success, it makes sense to never stop building on what sets you apart from others and helps you become your best you. Rath's *StrengthsFinders* is a commonly used tool to identify strengths. It's useful because its language is straightforward. Myers-Briggs is also commonly used, but because it relates primarily to personality type, it can be awkward to use in conversation ("Oh, I'm an INTJ"). *StrengthsFinders* easily resonates with others in terms of what you can do and how you'll do it, without a long training session on how to interpret it.

Both strengths and weaknesses are inevitable and unavoidable; we all have them. But focusing on our weaknesses while ignoring our strengths takes our focus away from becoming our best. Instead, knowing and applying your unique strengths and setting your goals in line with them will lead to more effective and more satisfying work.

Step 3: How Do You Manage Stress?

Stress can have one of the most insidious impacts on your performance and your career if it's not managed. Stress can come in many forms, including too much challenging work, too much boring work, dysfunctional teams, layoffs, large-scale change, economic uncertainty, work/life imbalance, bad bosses, and more. Since stress is unavoidable, learning how to deal with it is key to the self-control necessary to being an effective leader. It's important to figure out what your stress triggers are, understand what you can control, and learn to deal with what you can't. When under stress, we tend to revert to our unique stress behaviors; these reactions are different for everyone. Being aware of what those behaviors are for you is the first step. When you know what triggers your stress and how you generally react, you can self-monitor to improve your chances of managing your reactions more effectively. You can then focus on making subtle adjustments within yourself to improve your reaction, instead of attempting the fruitless task of trying to change others.

Self-control, especially under stress when it is most difficult, is a pillar for emotional intelligence, which we'll cover in chapter 7. Remember the rewards you'll receive from a more thoughtful reaction: a more favorable outcome and others viewing you more positively. If, however, the cause of stress stems from acting out of line with your core values, then you must immediately start taking active steps to address it. Too many times when our core values are challenged, we don't say anything, and stress festers. One small action could be the beginning of speaking up in ways that gradually feel more comfortable.

Author's Note (Christine): The stress of dealing with unethical people or situations has had a profound effect on me throughout my career. It started as a flicker, but throughout the years, when I didn't address it right away, it changed my personality...literally. I was blessed in that I finally noticed the need to pay attention to these challenges to my core values, finally listening to others who told me I needed to face them head on. You have to find a way to say something, first to a trusted friend or colleague, then to someone who can actually help. Better yet, if you have the ability and courage to do so, confront the unethical person. Always trust yourself, but also gather facts to state your case clearly, and remove emotion, focusing on the issue and impact and not on intent. Early in my career, I employed various means to be true to myself, including asking to be removed from an account and deciding to leave a company. Later, I moved into HR so I could be in a position to influence positive change more directly. I could never have known how much I'd be tested once I started serving in HR leadership roles, but by then the strong foundation I'd developed about my values helped me confront even greater challenges later.

Step 4: What Do Others See?

Rounding out our self-analysis is obtaining and utilizing objective feedback from others. To get a full picture of ourselves, we need input about how we're perceived by others and our impact on them to find both the consistencies and inconsistencies from our self-analysis. If you happen to be one of the fortunate few who gets specific, meaningful feedback from your supervisor, consider that one of the greatest gifts you'll receive in your leadership journey. Frequently, however, performance review feedback is too infrequent or vague to provide meaningful direction.

You can also perform a 360 degree feedback process. Also known as multi-rater feedback, the 360 degree feedback process involves gathering performance-related feedback from a variety of sources, including your boss, your peers, and your direct reports. If a formal 360 process isn't available, you can perform an informal 360 in the form of "Stop, Start, Continue."

1. Ask your boss, HR manager, or other neutral party to send an e-mail to a group that you work directly with, which includes peers, subordinates, and supervisors. Also include project team members from other teams you may have worked with.

2. Have the e-mail introduce the fact that you're seeking feedback for development purposes, and ask the questions, "What should X stop, what should X start, and what should X continue?" If your facilitator can provide respondents with context in which to situate their answers, such as your organization's leadership model, even better.

3. Finally, have the facilitator include an open-ended question, such as, "Please give one example of when X exhibited his/her best leadership skills," or, "Is there anything else you would like X to know about his/her leadership style?"

Finally, don't underestimate the importance of informal feedback...it's the kind you'll receive the most. You receive direct feedback when someone tells you you've done a good job or takes issue with something you've done. Indirect feedback requires you to be observant, watching for the subtle (or sometimes not-so-subtle) clues that others give you. Every reaction by others, including both verbal messages and nonverbal body language, is valuable feedback. Pay attention to the response you get to each interaction or presentation. Did it go well, or did it miss the mark? Specifically, what did others seem to react to well/poorly? Why do you think that might be? We usually get accurate feedback from informal responses if we're willing to pay attention, even if we're not fully sure what caused the response. Form a habit of reflection when something goes particularly well or particularly poorly, in order to understand what you can learn from it; it will provide valuable input over time to help you improve as a leader.

> *Author's Note (Kelly): Early in my career managing others, a clerical employee on my team came into my office one day, closed my door, and sat down across from me. She opened with, "I think you should know what people are saying about you." I no longer remember the specific feedback she gave me; I only remember that it was my first time receiving candid feedback from someone who reported to me, and I did indeed need to hear what she had to say. I remember taking it to heart, as the consequences of my actions were unintended. And in that moment, I learned the value of candid feedback. I've only had a handful of direct reports who've been willing to give me candid feedback, and I've been grateful for every single one of them who had the courage to do so. I've always listened carefully, then thanked them and told them how valuable it was to me, always hoping they'd continue the practice.*

Step 5: How Can You Serve Others?

You might wonder why the topic of serving others is part of the process of knowing yourself. As a leader, you have a significant opportunity to serve others. Unless your goals are solely about your own personal rewards, using your opportunity as a leader to help others can make your work far more rewarding. An additional—and significant—side benefit is that serving others can also help reduce the impact of stress, especially when that stress is due to circumstances outside of our control. Focusing on others can lessen our focus on the difficult things in our own lives. Also, leaders who help others along the way have a better reputation than those who focus solely on their own agendas. Serving others as a leader is truly a win-win, with no downside.

> *Author's Note (Kelly): I'd been leading others for a while and had gotten involved in my company's diversity effort. I was making a passionate plea to a senior executive for a diversity mentoring program, when he respectfully asked me what I'd done in that regard lately. I stammered into shamed silence and vowed that never again would I fail to have an answer to that question. That week, I began inviting employees of diverse backgrounds in our male-dominated company to lunch. I became accustomed to their initial awkward response, as we often barely knew each other, and I could sense that they wondered what my agenda was. I got used to an uncomfortable first lunch,*

but always invited them to a second. I learned not to be surprised that often the second lunch felt like we were old friends. A few of these relationships didn't survive a third or fourth lunch, but many of them have survived for decades. From that executive's challenge, I learned that I have a passion for mentoring, coaching, and developing others. His question is one of the greatest gifts I've ever received.

Step 6: What Do You Stand For?

The foundation on a journey to knowing yourself concludes with an understanding of your core values. Whether or not you're aware of them, your values guide all of your actions. They tell you whether you'll be a fit with your organization's culture: that is, whether you share the same values. You'll need to constantly shift and change with the needs of your organizations and of those around you, and some of those shifts will test your values. Stress is often an indicator that your values are being tested; it can be difficult to be your best self at these times. You must constantly decide what really matters to you, and keep it in front of you. Doing so will inspire others. The five-minute core values exercise at the end of this chapter is your starting point to knowing yourself. We promise, it's not your usual approach to this topic.

Author's Note (Christine): My values journey has taken years and is ongoing. But I will say, it took just this one time to stand up to something that wasn't in line with one of my values of treating people honestly and with respect, and from that moment on I never turned back. I remember it like it was yesterday: a situation in which there was a severe lack of integrity and accountability, and, the environment being what it was, nobody had said a word. During an acquisition when I was in an integration HR role, a leader made a flippant comment about the hundreds of low performers he could get rid of. This comment gradually turned into a target for the organization to meet. I made clear to the particular leaders whom I supported that, unless they had a history of documentation regarding the said "low performers," we would not be letting people go. Rather, we'd follow a legal process to identify jobs to eliminate and evaluate people based on their skills. After some debate with my leaders and HR peers, it was agreed that we would manage employees' performance in the usual manner and have a separate process for job elimination to create the go-forward organization. I felt that going against a prominent leader from the acquiring company and essentially campaigning with my HR peers might cost me my job. We all risked a lot, given that the expectation for layoffs was "hundreds," and we actually eliminated nowhere near that. Layoffs are a painful, inevitable reality of mergers and acquisitions. But in this case, employees ended up being treated fairly through a sound, legally defensible process. Ultimately, that leader was held accountable for making such broad, insensitive comments, and we were viewed as having done the right thing. This success aside, however, many other times where I've led with my values, I felt quite alone. But I knew others were watching and that I was being true to myself.

It's Like Getting a Coach

The small investment of time to know yourself, to truly understand your values and discover your unique leadership capabilities, is the foundation to making an impact where you are today and to quickly adapting to increased leadership complexity as you advance. To use a sailing metaphor, you may continue to be cast adrift, asking, "How did I get here?" Or, instead, you can confidently hoist up the sail of knowing yourself, and head for the destination of your choosing.

* * *

Additional Resources

What You're Really Meant to Do: A Road Map for Reaching Your Unique Potential, by Robert Steven Kaplan (Harvard Business Review Press, 2013).

Centered Leadership: Leading with Purpose, Clarity, and Impact, by Joanna Barsh and Johanne Lavoie (Crown Business, 2014).

StrengthsFinders 2.0, by Tom Rath (Gallup Press, 2007).

Myers-Briggs Type Indicator, http://www.myersbriggs.org/my-mbti-personality-type/mbti-basics/.

The Center for Ethical Leadership core values exercises and resources, http://www.ethicalleadership.org/uploads/2/6/2/6/26265761/1.4_core_values_exercise.pdf.

Leadership Companion Exercise: Knowing Yourself

Assess

Step 1: What Inspires You?

1. Think back to a time you were most proud of yourself. Why did you feel proud?

   _____

   _____

   _____

2. Think of a person who inspires you. List his or her attributes that make you feel that way.

   _____

   _____

   _____

3. Think of the last time you were really excited about something. (Go as far back as necessary.) Why did you feel excited?

   _____

   _____

Step 2: What Are Your Peak Moments?

4. Write down three to five times in your life when you were your most authentic and best self (list the first

times that come to mind; don't think too hard about it). Write a short description of what happened for each, considering such factors as:

a. Were you alone or in a crowd?
b. What was the challenge you were facing?
c. Why was it a peak moment?
d. What was your role?
e. How did you overcome challenges?
f. What are you particularly proud of?[6]

Peak Moment #1:

_____

_____

_____

Peak Moment #2:

_____

_____

_____

Peak Moment #3:

_____

_____

_____

Step 3: What Are My Strengths?

5. Building on the information gained in the peak moments exercise, think of five strengths you used in those peak moments.

a. _____

b. _____

c. _____

d. _____

e. _____

6. What strengths have others, including teachers, parents, friends, supervisors, coworkers, and mentors, identified in you?

_____

_____

_____

Step 4: What Are Your Stress Triggers?

7. Identifying the cause of stress simply takes a small effort of awareness. For a few days or up to a week, jot down your answers to these questions:

a. What made you angry, frustrated, or sad today?

b. In what parts of your body do you currently feel pain, tension, or tightness?

c. What past event does this reaction relate to?

d. What core value(s) does this reaction relate to?

e. Is this important enough to take away your happiness, to make you off center?

f. Choice: What one action will I take to prevent reacting to this trigger in the future?

8. Reflect on your answers to these questions to identify common stress triggers and your typical responses to them, as well as tactics you can take to reduce your reaction.

Step 5: How Can I Serve Others?

9. The *Fortune* article "10 Ways to Help Others That Will Lead You to Success" provides examples of ways you can help others in a workplace setting.[7] Think about the one or two actions that are the best fit for your passions, personality, and the opportunities routinely available to you:

    a. Sharing knowledge
    b. Finding out what's valuable to others
    c. Sharing your resources
    d. Making others aware of an opportunity
    e. Providing transparent feedback
    f. Being an advocate
    g. Giving introductions
    h. Volunteering your time
    i. Recognizing others
    j. Giving of your gifts

Step 6: Core Values Exercise[8]

10. Spend five minutes freewriting responses to the following two statements. Try to keep writing that entire time, without judging or editing what you're writing.

Its open-endedness is what makes it most effective, because it encourages your unique, unprompted responses.

a. Describe things throughout your life you've consistently believed. "I believe…"

_____

_____

_____

b. Describe your ideal life (career, family, friends, hobbies, learning, anything that's meaningful to you). "My ideal life looks like…"

_____

_____

_____

When you're finished, circle or highlight key words or statements that articulate your core values.

11. If it's too challenging to identify your own personal values, think of someone who you admire and respect and describe why. It's likely that you respect and admire them because their values are similar to yours.

_____

_____

_____

Adapt

12. What were the most surprising things that came up in
    these exercises?

    _____

    _____

    _____

13. What, if any, common themes emerge?

    _____

    _____

    _____

CHAPTER 3

Knowing Others

Self-knowledge comes from
knowing other men.
—Johann Wolfgang von Goethe

How You Show Up

Every interaction with others is an opportunity to bring out your unique leadership qualities and to address the other 50 percent of the self-leadership equation: how you show up to others. By being aware of how you show up, you begin the important work of developing the emotional intelligence now considered critical for effective leadership. The goal isn't to show up as something new or different than you really are; the goal is to bring your best self into every interaction naturally. In this chapter, we'll guide you through several topics to accomplish this, including organizational culture, knowing your team, effective communication, understanding non-verbals, conflict management, and networking.

How Work Gets Done around Here

How do you define culture? *Inc. Magazine's* encyclopedia defines it this way: "Corporate culture refers to the shared values, attitudes, standards, and beliefs that characterize members of an organization and define its nature. Corporate culture is rooted in an organization's goals, strategies, structure, and approaches to labor, customers, investors, and the greater community."[9]

How do you describe the culture of your organization? Maybe your organization tangibly states its culture. While that's a place to start, be careful not to assume that the official version, with its banners and tchotchkes, is the full picture: companies often go to great lengths to describe what they *wish* to be versus what they actually *are*. Culture is why so many acquisitions fail: unstated or underestimated culture differences always trump official organizational charts, mission statements, and stated "go forward" cultures. That's because culture is a mass series of habits and behaviors of which we are largely unaware.

To figure out the culture in which you find yourself, start with one simple question: How does work get done around here? More specifically, in the *Inc. Magazine* article "Perception vs. Reality: Do You Know What Your Real Company Culture Is?" Jim Arena, workplace culture expert, stated, "It is the invisible hand that accelerates and decelerates your company strategy. The strength of your culture is actually determined by how well aligned it is to your strategy."[10]

How might you define how work gets done in your company? There's an exercise about culture at the end of this chapter. The goal is to combine your unique qualities with your company's cultural attributes in order to be the most effective at getting things done and to gain awareness of the gaps that exist between your style and your organization's culture.

Knowing the Team

Next, there's understanding the impact of your immediate team's dynamics. Where is there common ground on the team? Where is there conflict? How does that impact your job? What topics are safe to talk about and what are the "elephants in the room"? What are some nonthreatening ways to approach those off-limits topics? A solid understanding of team norms and rules is crucial to knowing how to effectively navigate as part of the team. By answering these questions and having a clear picture of the team's dynamics, over time you can lead the team, either formally or informally, pushing change and honest conversation at a tolerable rate and always bringing the team back to its common purpose. By depersonalizing discussions within the team, you can help put everyone's ideas and experiences on a level playing field. By articulating your team's dynamics, you can become more aware of the role you play on the team, and, more importantly, of the role you want to play.

Make an Impact Right Now: Communication Checklist for Leaders
The following are quick and easy steps to follow when doing any important communication.

1. What is the goal of this communication?
   Some examples may be asking for help, tactical directives, or getting buy-in to an idea or concept.
2. Who is your audience?
3. What form of communication is best for your audience?
   For topics that are early in their development, new to your audience, or controversial, a conversation is best, whereas FYIs, updates, or tactical requests are better in writing.
4. "Just tell me what you want me to do."
   Be specific, stating requests at the beginning and repeating them at the end.
5. Check your work.
   Nothing ruins leadership credibility like a communication with silly typos and confusing directions. Always double-check your communications before sending. Even better, have someone else review your communication if the message is complex, the stakes are high, or it's important to manage your brand with the audience.
6. Be nice.
   Common courtesy goes a long way in today's hectic environment. Saying "please" and "thank you" and expressing empathy to your audience shows that you care, which builds trust.

7. Repeat, repeat, repeat.

    Just because you communicated something doesn't mean that people heard your message, understood it, or followed through. Build in frequency to ensure that you communicate to your audience several times and in different ways, depending on the message's importance. Follow up to ensure that you understand barriers.

Did You Just Roll Your Eyes at Me?

Peter Drucker's famous quote says it all: "The most important thing in communication is hearing what isn't being said." The spoken word is overrated. Particularly in a corporate environment with multiple stakeholders, what people say is often not what they actually mean. Two back-to-back studies done in 1967 (Mehrabian and Wiener, 1967, and Mehrabian and Ferris, 1967) combined into what resulted in the 55/38/7 formula: communication is 55 percent body language, 38 percent tone of voice, and 7 percent actual words spoken.[11] Being aware of body language and its meaning, in others as well as in you, plays a crucial role in helping you manage how you want to show up and in more accurately assessing team dynamics. Through this awareness, you can lead through the discrepancies between what's being said and not said, by asking follow-up questions to clarify or by encouraging more discussion. Below are a few unspoken messages, along with their common nonverbal signs:

Message	Nonverbal Signs
Showing respect	Making eye contact, not interrupting, asking questions, putting away laptops and mobile devices
On board with the topic, ready to serve as a supporter or champion	Sitting upright, nodding, making eye contact, smiling, asking follow-on questions, making supportive statements
Individual is trustworthy	Learning forward, open arms
Doesn't like the direction	Arms folded, rolling eyes, leaning back
Boredom, feeling that the meeting is over or not adding value	Checking electronic devices, blank stares, watching the clock

Organizations that tolerate disrespectful nonverbals such as eye-rolling and obvious dismissiveness won't be atmospheres in which people can thrive and grow. In the frequently cited book *The Seven Principles for Making Marriage Work: A Practical Guide from the Country's Foremost Relationship Expert*, eye-rolling between spouses is a leading predictor of a failed marriage—along with sneering, mockery, and hostile humor. Eye rolling is considered the ultimate showing of disrespect and is poisonous to relationships because it conveys disgust.[12] It isn't any less serious in the workplace.

Having Courage in Conversations

A significant part of knowing others is managing inevitable conflict. Some conflict is healthy, such as when competing organizational objectives can help push the organization to optimal results. Unhealthy conflict, however, especially when unresolved, festers and becomes destructive. Either fear or unclear expectations is generally at the heart of any conflict. Often, the participants don't fully realize the true nature of the conflict. Consider the possibility that there may be multiple causes and that you can shorten or even eliminate the conflict. Remember that everyone brings his or her specific lens and past experiences into every interaction, potentially causing misunderstandings with others who bring *their* specific lenses and unique past experiences. It's also common to assume that conflict is about us: taking things personally is a natural response to conflict. The way people act in a situation likely stems from their experiences, or what happened that morning, and often isn't about us at all.

These four steps will help drive courage in any conversation:

1. **Know yourself first.** Consider why a particular topic triggers an emotional reaction in you and reflect on past

examples. Have the conversation you wish to have with yourself first before confronting the individual(s), being sure you know the true source of your own distress and the desired outcome.

Example: "Trust in people with whom I work is very important to me. When someone on the team triangulates and goes around me to address a problem, that feels disrespectful and counterproductive."

2. **Talk to them!** Seek to understand the heart of the issue: the other person's perspective matters as much as yours. Especially listen for the underlying expectation they have which you're not meeting; search inside yourself for the same. Frame your perspective in how it makes you feel, not your assumption of their intent; you can only be sure of your own feelings, and it's difficult for someone to argue how you're feeling. They can (and likely will) be defensive if you assume what they meant, especially if it's negative.

    Example: "I place a huge value on the quality and consistency of my work and the trust of my colleagues, so you going around me to address this issue really upset me."

3. **Find common ground.** Understand the stakes, interests, and priorities for each party. Where do yours and theirs meet?

    Example: "What is most important to you with this issue? This is what is most important to me."

4. **Commit to an approach.** Live up to the commitment you make.

Example: "Thank you for being open with me. In the future can you please take the time to bring in my team to ensure the best response? If our team has not provided adequate service in the past, then please bring that to my attention."

Networking: Its Awkward Days Are Over

It's broadly accepted that networking is very important to your career. Porter Gale equates networking to personal wealth with her book, "Your Network is Your Net Worth." But why? And why does it sometimes have a negative reputation? Networking can help you be more successful when it builds relationships to get more work done, more effectively, for your organization. It gets a bad reputation when it feels awkward or when the perception is that its sole purpose is to lobby for a new job or to curry favor with superiors. Some organizational cultures support networking, encouraging employees to schedule brief networking interviews with potential hiring managers to understand what roles in their area look like and what experiences are required. In other organizations, it's viewed as disloyalty or a waste of time. It's best to first know your organization's culture and how it views networking. If formal networking is viewed negatively, there are still ways to accomplish most of the same goals. You can volunteer for projects that will give you exposure to other leaders and teams. You can indicate your interest in another area of your organization and share it with your boss as part of your development plan, opening the door for your boss's introduction to other hiring managers. You can become involved in extracurricular activities such as community involvement, which will gain you new exposure. The main thing is to get out there and get known. Too many great leaders languish in a small corner of their organization, not because they're incapable of more, but because others don't know what they're capable of. Doing good work is still table stakes, but a little marketing of "the product of you" is generally necessary to ensure you reach your potential. Knowing others also means making sure that they know you.

* * *

Additional Resources

The Definitive Book of Body Language: The Hidden Meaning behind People's Gestures and Expressions, by Barbara Pease (Bantam, 2006).

How to Get Your Point Across in 30 Seconds or Less, by Milo O. Frank (Gallery Books, 1990).

Crucial Conversations: Tools for Talking When Stakes Are High, by Kerry Patterson, Joseph Grenny, Ron McMillan, and Al Switzler (McGraw-Hill, 2011).

Your Network Is Your Net Worth: Unlock the Hidden Power of Connections for Wealth, Success, and Happiness in the Digital Age, by Porter Gale (Atria Books, 2013).

Leadership Companion Exercise: Knowing Others

Assess

Answer the following questions.

1. Culture: How does work get done in your organization?
   a. What is the stated culture of your organization?
   b. What one or two words would you use to describe the culture? Is your experience in the culture different from what's stated?
   c. Does your company have a well-communicated strategy?
   d. How does your company execute work (e.g., through strict processes, knowing certain people, informal or formal communication channels)?
   e. How does work get prioritized?
   f. How would you describe the dominant leadership style?
   g. What stories do people tell about work getting done?

   _____
   _____
   _____
   _____
   _____

2. Reflect on the Knowing Yourself exercises from chapter 2. How are your strengths, core values, etc., consistent with the culture? How are they opposed?

_____

_____

_____

_____

_____

3. Knowing the Team: How can I lead on my team?
   a. Who are the informal versus the formal leaders?
   b. Are there toxic people on my team? If so, what effect do they have?
   c. Does your team make decisions collectively?
   d. Does your team set goals together?
   e. Does your team meet regularly? What is the content of those meetings (sharing status, making decisions, discussing problems)?
   f. What style, skill, or strength do you bring to your team?
   g. What is your role on your team (passive contributor, negotiator, project manager)?

_____

_____

_____

4. Nonverbals
   a. Which nonverbal signals do you frequently notice in others?

b. Which nonverbal signals do you most frequently demonstrate?

c. What triggers those nonverbal signals?

d. What messages do you believe they send to those you are with?

_____

_____

_____

5. Active Networking

   a. Make a list of five people with whom you need to have a positive relationship to achieve your career goals. For each, write one way that would be comfortable for you to reach out to them.

      i. _____

      ii. _____

      iii. _____

      iv. _____

      v. _____

   b. Name one person who inspires you in some way. Can you share with him or her why?

   _____

   _____

   c. Name one person who needs a helping hand, a mentor, or advice. How can you help?

   _____

   _____

d. Name one person to whom you owe a "thank-you" for providing help, knowledge, or support. How can you thank him or her?

_____

_____

Adapt

Culture

6. Pick one strength you have which you can leverage in your organization's culture, and identify how you will do so.

_____

_____

_____

Team

7. Reflect on your Knowing Yourself information in the context of the team dynamics you've identified: what one or two ways can you lead on the team to make it higher performing?

_____

_____

_____

Communication

8. Create a mini-communication plan using this chapter's "Communication Checklist for Leaders." Choose something simple going on right now on which you can practice the relevant communication tips.

_____

_____

_____

Nonverbals

9. Which nonverbal signal that you employ has the greatest negative consequences to you? Commit to keeping watch on this nonverbal for the next thirty days.

_____

_____

_____

Courage in Conversations

10. Think of a recent conversation that didn't go as well as you'd have liked. What could you do differently next time to achieve a more positive result?

_____

_____

_____

Leading Others

LEADING OTHERS: A PREVIEW

Leadership is the art of getting someone
else to do something you want done,
because he wants to do it.
—Dwight D. Eisenhower

eading others is a step change in complexity over simply leading yourself, as you now must directly manage the performance and motivation of others who are wired differently than you are. In Knowing Others, you gained the benefits from understanding others. When directly managing others, your focus must shift outward: knowing others now means that you must benefit the people you lead. You're no longer in complete control of all of the outcomes, although your actions as the leader will definitely have an impact—positively, negatively, or even both—perhaps affecting different team members differently. Supervisors have a big impact on people and are often the single biggest reason employees either stay with or leave a company.

To be the kind of leader whom talented people want to follow, you'll need to draw heavily on your foundation of knowing yourself and knowing others. Combining that foundation with fundamentals of what people really want from a leader will immediately set you on the right path. We'll introduce the concept of authority, as understanding the different types of authority helps set the stage for the important skill of influencing. We'll explore employee engagement in chapter 5. Finally, your role is to coach those on your team for higher performance. Given your power as their supervisor, and given your employees' vulnerability when they need constructive criticism, approaching this responsibility factually but with sensitivity is a critical skill to maintaining their engagement. Coaching is too often avoided, as many supervisors lack the skill or don't like conflict. This robs employees of valuable opportunities to improve and limits the performance of the team and the organization, ultimately hurting their supervisor (you). Chapter 6 examines effective coaching techniques that can be performed with minimal time and effort.

With a strong foundation in knowing yourself and knowing others, a good understanding of how authority works and what engages employees, and equipped with effective coaching techniques, you can be a positive leader people want to work for. Your team will perform well, which means that you, as supervisor, will perform well, too. This will not only help your career, but you'll also enjoy the satisfaction of having a positive impact on others.

CHAPTER 4

Leadership Fundamentals and Authority

No man has any natural authority
over his fellow men.

—Jean-Jacques Rousseau

What Do People Want in a Leader?

A Gallup study asked more than ten thousand people why they follow the most influential leader in their lives. The study found that the most effective leaders always: 1) invest in their strengths; 2) surround themselves with the right people and then maximize the performance of their team; and 3) understand their followers' needs.[13]

Researching the traits followers want in their leaders produces multiple lists, but there are some common themes across them. From our experience, neither these traits nor those needed at higher levels of leadership complexity, as described in later chapters, are inherent behaviors that you're "born with." Instead, they're completely actionable. You simply apply your unique leadership qualities to these actions: trust, vision, execution, and caring.

Trust

Building trust with employees is a critical responsibility for leaders.[14] Trust has two components: competence and reliability. For people to trust you, they first must believe that you're able to do what they want or need done, and then they must have reason to believe that you'll actually do it. It's important, when you're new to a team, to acknowledge that it takes time to build trust. Anything you can do as a new leader to accelerate building trust with your team will correspondingly accelerate your team's opportunity to perform well. To trust you, your team needs to see consistent behavior from you, proving to them that you're acting in their best interests. No matter how high up the ladder you go, you start over every time, building trust with every new team and new team member. Forgetting or getting frustrated by this necessity is a mistake that even many experienced leaders make.

The concept of servant leadership fits neatly into a discussion of trust, since it's an effective way of demonstrating that you're acting in the team's best interest and not just your own. Key features of servant leadership include good listening skills and the empathy first to understand and then to meet your employees' needs. Servant leaders honor unspoken employee requests:

1. Hear me and understand me.
2. Even if you disagree with me, please don't make me wrong.
3. Acknowledge the greatness within me.
4. Remember to look for my loving intentions.
5. Tell me the truth with compassion.[15]

Effective leaders always remember that it's their responsibility to build trust with their team and to meet their individual needs as much as possible, while also meeting the needs of the organization.

Vision

Followers want a worthwhile target. Effective leaders define and communicate an inspiring vision that's meaningful and aspirational, a vision worth stretching toward. To motivate others toward your vision, you'll need to be positive and able to clearly communicate why it's a worthy endeavor. People often don't like change, so it's best if you can involve your team in creating the vision. As their leader, you need the ability to move them away from what is familiar, by explaining why the change is necessary and inspiring them to make the changes needed. You may also need to soothe any anxieties they have about whether they're equipped to make the change.

Author's Note (Christine): While leading a team through our annual planning, we discussed a vision for our team. What truly aspirational thing did we want to be? The notion of being sought out to help solve problems even before they were problems came up. The vision statement turned into "We are indispensable partners to our internal customers." We discussed what this would look like, how each team member would feel, and what customers would say. We constructed an action plan that we believed would encourage this notion of indispensability. A year later, we went back and looked at the vision and the plan and took an inventory of all we'd accomplished...we couldn't believe how far we'd come! The things that were issues for us the prior year came off our list, and, based on casual discussions with our customers over the year, the team felt that they were, indeed, becoming literally "indispensable."

Execution

Employees want to follow leaders who are competent and can execute...in short, they want to follow winners. In the long run, it isn't very inspirational to follow someone who isn't leading you anywhere. Your ability to follow through also suggests that you have other leadership qualities, including the commitment and courage to persevere in the face of challenge. Winners don't quit.

Caring

Finally, people care about more than just accomplishing goals—they also care *how* goals are achieved. It isn't enough just to get things done; your employees will pay attention to how you've treated them along the way. Followers want leaders who care. They want you as their leader to learn about each of them as individuals, understand what their goals are, and discover what's important to them in their personal lives. They want to be treated with basic human dignity and respect. They want a humble leader, one who'll give credit where it's deserved and who'll compensate them fairly for their contribution. They want a transparent leader who values them enough to listen to them and to communicate to them as much and as often as is appropriate, appreciating their need for information about what impacts them. It isn't a coincidence that these traits sound like a leader who can be trusted. Employees won't trust leaders who care only about themselves.

In summary, effective leaders set a vision and then inspire their teams to accomplish it. Their followers are motivated by how they do what they do, following someone who cares about them and who demonstrates trust through humility and service. Their teams accomplish much, for themselves and the organization. And they stay.

The Importance of Adaptability

Why is adaptability important in a leader? Leaders find themselves in a variety of circumstances, interacting with a diverse range of people. An approach or behavior successful in one circumstance or with one group of people won't necessarily be successful with the next one. The ability to adapt to different situations starts with a keen understanding of yourself and others, as discussed in previous chapters. Your teammates will notice and appreciate your ability to adjust your approach to fit their needs. For example, an experienced employee may resent the detailed direction needed by a more junior employee. You'll also want to adapt your approach based on the overall situation. A crisis or a fast-paced, complex project may require significantly more of your direct involvement than does a stable environment. Explaining why you're providing more direction in these circumstances will help keep your team from resenting what could be seen as a lack of trust in them, especially if they're an experienced team or you normally take a more hands-off approach.

It's important, however, not to overadapt. Most of us have been in situations where we felt as though we needed to act like someone we're not. Remember how that made you feel? It can be exhausting to act outside of your genuine self, and others can usually sense that something is "off" when you do. Developing an adaptable style means experimenting over time to find practices and actions that meet the needs of your team, while still being authentic to your natural style. An example is that introverts often aren't comfortable acting like extroverts, but they can develop extrovert-like actions and habits that become comfortable with practice over time.

Soon, you'll be able to flex your approach, seamlessly adjusting as the team and the situation requires. You aren't changing who you are: your core self, beliefs, and values. Rather, you're adjusting what you do, meeting others' needs and building their trust.

Author's Note (Kelly): As an introvert, I've had to force myself to develop the habit of walking around. Much of the time I'd rather be head-down in my office, getting work done. But as the leader, I know it's important to be visible with the team and show them that they matter as individuals. I first really learned this when the bulk of my team was in another city. I tried to travel there once a month for a couple of days. The day I arrived, I always spent at least the first two hours just walking the office, greeting each of the forty employees and making small talk. It always felt like a waste of time, except in my gut I knew that it wasn't. That the boss would invest that kind of time in them was very much noticed by the team. I'm still friends with many of them a decade later, selfishly grateful that I got to know them. I carried that learning into my next assignment, where I was part of leadership for a global team of sixty-five. Though the group was large and most of them didn't report directly to me, I again made myself walk the entire floor each Monday, and once again I was grateful, this time for the opportunity to get to know this diverse group over the two years I was part of the team. Halfway through my tenure, a peer (and fellow introvert) on the leadership team asked me how I'd been able to develop such strong relationships with the larger team so quickly. I happily shared my super-easy "secret." Though he acknowledged it was a good idea, he didn't follow suit. I viewed it as his loss.

Title Alone Does Not Make You a Leader— Authority Explained

The American Heritage Dictionary defines authority as "power as-signed to another." Direct power, or the authority that your organi-zation has formally granted you, is what most people think of first when they think of authority. But that same dictionary provides an-other definition of authority as the "power to *influence or persuade* (emphasis added) resulting from knowledge or experience."[16] This informal authority can be far more powerful for leaders than the formal authority granted by their position. Formal authority brings with it the powers of the office; informal authority gives you the subtle yet substantial power to influence others and extend your reach way beyond the limits of your job description.[17] Formal, posi-tional power is generally effective in the short-term, but can be less effective in the long run for retaining and growing the best people and at moving employees to give their best. After all, who wants to work for very long simply out of fear of losing their job?

Sources of Authority

The formal authority that comes with your position is only one source of authority. It's the most basic form of authority and, as we said, perhaps the least effective in the long term.

Because different people have different values and needs, they'll respond to different sources of authority to different degrees.

One examination of sources of authority is Hersey, Blanchard, and Johnson in their book *Management of Organizational Behavior*, first published in 1969. They explored seven sources of authority, both formal and informal:

Formal (Positional) Authority

1. Legitimate power
2. Reward power
3. Coercive power

Informal (Influential) Authority

4. Expert power
5. Information power
6. Connection power
7. Referent power

Formal authority is the power from your role as leader. Of these powers, legitimate power, which results from the perception of others that you have the authority to make decisions based on your role as the leader, is the most straightforward.[18] Reward power is your ability to provide things people would like to have,[19] while coercive power is your ability to deliver punishment or consequences.[20] (These are commonly referred to as the "carrot" and the "stick" in terms of how to get things done.) All leaders have some degree of these formal authorities as a result of their roles.

Informal sources of authority come from your expertise, influence, or personality. Expert power comes from others' positive perceptions of your education, experience, or expertise.[21] An example is that most people will rely heavily on the opinion of experts in tax or law based on their expertise for decisions in those areas. Information power and connection power draw from the perception that you have access to or control of useful information[22] and from your relationships with influential people and organizations.[23] Finally, referent power is your ability to get others to follow you based on how much you are admired or respected.[24] Your ability to draw on these informal sources of authority, perhaps several at the same time, will depend on your experiences and your natural style. Being aware of all of them helps you to build and leverage as many as possible over time, to become more effective in encouraging others to follow you.

Leadership is the art of getting others to follow you. Authority is the related concept of power. While they're obviously directly linked, the best leaders have learned that the less they rely on formal authority, the more effective they are. Learning to develop skills that will encourage others to follow you, without leaning on formal authority, will help you make an impact in whatever your role, at all levels.

* * *

Additional Resources

Servant Leadership: A Journey into the Nature of Legitimate Power and Greatness, by Robert K. Greenleaf (Paulist Press, 2002).

Leadership and the One Minute Manager Updated Ed: Increasing Effectiveness through Situational Leadership II, by Ken Blanchard (William Morrow, 2013).

Good to Great: Why Some Companies Make the Leap and Others Don't, by Jim Collins (Harper Business, 2001).

The Introvert Advantage: How Quiet People Can Thrive in an Extrovert World, by Marti Olsen Laney, Psy.D. (Workman Publishing Company, 2002).

Leadership Companion Exercise: Leadership Fundamentals and Authority

Assess

1. Which of the informal sources of authority—expert, information, connection, and referent—are already strengths for you? Which of them can you develop over time and how?

   _____

   _____

   _____

2. Which of the themes listed in "What Do People Want in a Leader?" resonated with you the most? Why?

   _____

   _____

   _____

Adapt

3. Name a meeting, person, or project to which you can apply a new leadership approach. How will you approach it? How will you get feedback?

   _____

   _____

   _____

Scaling for Organizations

Share the informal sources of authority with each of your team members. Discuss which ones are natural to them and how they can develop additional sources as strengths.

CHAPTER 5

Engaging and Retaining Others

People don't care how much you know
until they know how much you care.

–John C. Maxwell

What Is Employee Engagement and Why Is It Important?

As a leader, it's important to understand what employee engagement is and how to drive it. Put simply by Kevin Kruse in a *Forbes* article, "Employee engagement is the emotional commitment the employee has to the organization and its goals."[25] Note, it doesn't mean happiness or satisfaction. While happiness and satisfaction on the job are positive, they don't necessarily result in the extra performance or effort that true employee engagement can generate. "When employees care—when they are engaged—they use discretionary effort."[26]

Keeping with the "knowing yourself" theme, it's important to understand what engages you as an employee, then as a leader responsible for your team's engagement, to learn what drives the team's performance and yours. You may also be asked to help tackle employee engagement more broadly in your organization. Understanding what drives engagement will benefit you, your team, and your organization.

What Drives Engagement?

Just as there are many different surveys measuring employee engagement, there are multiple engagement models, all with their own lists of what they believe drives engagement. As the leader of your team, you have a significant impact on one overriding engagement driver: whether your employees feel valued. Do you have a positive relationship with your employees? Do you include them in what's going on? Do you focus on their career needs and goals? Do you show appreciation when deserved? These simple but often overlooked actions by managers can make the difference between engaged employees who are productive and stay and those who punch the clock and leave at the first good offer. Here are some additional ways to engage your employees and make them feel valued:

1. Foster open communication and trust with your people through regular touch points on projects, informal conversations, requests for input, and development/career discussions.

CHRISTINE MCLAREN AND KELLY MCCLEARY

2. Develop people through challenging team assignments or stretch projects.
3. Empower employees to act independently.
4. Set clear expectations.
5. Manage/deal with performance problems.
6. Ensure people's strengths are leveraged; sometimes poor performers are just in the wrong job.

Find ways to include your employees, get to know them and tap into their strengths, and help them feel appreciated in ways that fit your leadership style. Through trial and error, applying the principles of knowing others to understand their needs, and knowing yourself, you can develop natural habits that engage others.

The Engagement Survey "Trap"

It's important not to focus on driving to a high employee engagement score, but instead on using engagement survey results as a tool to start a dialogue with your team about how to improve the work environment. Just because your score is high doesn't mean you have high engagement. Similarly, just because the organization is performing well and people are staying doesn't mean that engagement is high. The bottom line is that there are many reasons for high scores, low scores, and everything in between. The true purpose of engagement surveys is to provide a starting point for a real discussion about issues in the organization and team and then doing something about it. Understanding what the organization should keep doing is equally important.

Many leaders are lulled into responding tactically to low scores on questions such as *We want more communication about what's going on, I don't get paid enough,* and *I have too much work.* Low scores to these questions may actually be your employees telling you, *Our culture rewards status quo versus creative risk-taking, My work doesn't fit my skills,* and *I don't feel valued,* and *I don't like my manager.* It's important to engage your employees to accurately interpret what they're really trying to tell you about the results.

It's also important not to over rely on engagement surveys. Compare the results to other organizational metrics, such as scorecards, talent assessments, performance reviews, and compensation data, to look for patterns among manager performance and talent status. Also consider the circumstances. For example, a new manager driving significant change may have lower scores. Survey results may provide a red flag for management issues. Are development and advancement opportunities lacking? Maybe you need more robust workforce plans to map future skills and need to create more opportunities. Look for patterns that will help you identify actions to improve the environment for your employees, get them performing, and make them want to stay.

Action Plans and Committees

If you're going to invest the time and energy to administer an engagement survey, it's important to be ready to take appropriate actions as a result. Failing to do so sends a strong signal to your team members that you didn't really value their feedback after all. Many organizations form committees and action plans to address results from their engagement surveys. Unfortunately, if you want to effectively address engagement issues, it's not that simple. Even committees with executive sponsorship can struggle to make improvements, because so many factors can drive the results. For example, let's say an organization scored low in communication, so it formed a communication team to put out regular communications regarding what's going on in the organization. However, the effort was ineffective, because what people really wanted to know had more to do with their day to day—who's leaving and who's coming, did my boss stop by and ask me about my weekend, does this new process threaten my job—all of which must be communicated by the supervisor, and not a committee. At worst, committees and action plans may be completely misdirected, based on assumptions about what drove the survey results, without any additional employee feedback or input.

Another common trend is handing over action planning to employees and managers lower in the organization. It does make sense to involve the troops in understanding the underlying messages they were trying to communicate.

However, don't completely delegate action planning, since employees may feel that any problems they've just communicated are being handed back to them by the very people who caused them and who actually have the ability to address them. Ideally, leaders will involve others in assessing what needs to be addressed but won't delegate action planning. Based on feedback from the team, leaders should decide on the one or two most important things needed to increase engagement. As leader, you must own the hard work of regularly communicating to and getting feedback from the team to monitor progress against your plans. Administering an abbreviated "check in" survey is another way to check midterm progress.

Picnics and Pinball Machines

It can be tempting to react to engagement survey results by implementing "fun" activities such as company picnics, jeans days, and game areas with pinball machines, pool tables, and dart boards. In one organization, employees complained about a restroom that had fallen into disrepair over the years, and the company invested in an upgrade. It's no wonder these actions are popular: they're typically inexpensive, visible, easy to implement and...well...who doesn't like to have some fun, particularly if it might increase engagement? By themselves, these superficial actions often don't result in any meaningful improvement in engagement, and if they're to have any incremental impact, they may be more effective if they're tied to an overall theme like recognition or customer service. For example, a recognition program that highlights achievement of organizational goals can be celebrated with jeans or a picnic. Upgrading the restroom can be part of an overall "healthy work environment" or a wellness goal. Standalone check-the-box picnics in hopes of increasing customer service can do more to make talented employees feel patronized than engaged. Sincere efforts, tied to a meaningful overall objective, generally have the most impact.

Now that you have an understanding of the importance of your role in driving employee engagement and have noted a few effective activities, you can drive engagement and encourage committed employees on your team who will give extra effort and who will stay. In the next chapter, we'll explore how to be an effective coach. This important skill can be one of the most impactful drivers of engagement.

* * *

Additional Resources

First, Break All the Rules: What the World's Greatest Managers Do Differently, by James K. Harter (Gallup Press, 2016).

Carrots and Sticks Don't Work: Build a Culture of Employee Engagement with the Principles of RESPECT, by Paul L. Marciano (McGraw-Hill Education, 2010).

Leadership Companion Exercise: Engaging and Retaining Others

Assess

1. Reflect on a time when you were truly engaged in something you were doing. What made it motivating? What role did others play in keeping you motivated?

   _____

   _____

   _____

2. Which of the six ways to engage your employees is most important to you personally? Which of those is most lacking in your current role? What can you change to help improve your engagement?

   _____

   _____

   _____

Adapt

3. Think of one team member who is critical to your success. Which of the six ways to engage your employees do you feel is most important to that person? What one action could you take to improve that for him or her?

    _____

    _____

    _____

Scaling for Organizations

Have a discussion with your team about what is working well in the team and what could improve the work environment and engagement.

CHAPTER 6

Coaching Others

*A coach is someone who tells you what you
don't want to hear, and has you see what
you don't want to see, so you can be who
you have always known you could be.*

–TOM LANDRY

To Coach or Not to Coach?

ook in any human resources library or leadership learning and development curriculum and you can almost count on finding a how-to on effective coaching. After all, coaching is critical, as every leader's job is to mobilize others to accomplish organizational goals. While some companies view coaching as so critical that they've defined competencies around coaching and require training in it for all supervisors, too many organizations fail to ensure that their leaders are effective coaches, or even that coaching takes place. Compounding the problem is the fact that coaching doesn't come naturally for many leaders, but it's a skill that can be developed. Some common obstacles to effective coaching include:

- Aversion to conflict
- Lack of trust
- Confusing tactical feedback with coaching toward goals and peak performance
- Perceived lack of time (though we'd argue that this time is often a proxy for lack of prioritization)

And yet, even with these obstacles and not enough effective coaching going on, the reality is that the work is still getting done, isn't it? Does coaching really have a measurable impact? Few would argue against the regular practice of coaching employees, but what's the burning platform for coaching? *Merriam-Webster* defines a coach simply as "someone who instructs or trains." Leadership is a complex task; few of us come fully equipped to the role. Coaching provides the constructive feedback necessary to help others tap their unique qualities.

Studies also show that most employees *want* feedback and will improve performance through coaching, versus the typical formal means such as performance reviews:

Research psychologists at Kansas State University, Eastern Kentucky University, and Texas A&M recently examined the effect on performance of negative feedback during annual performance reviews. Rather than motivating employees to improve, they found it had the opposite effect. In fact, many employees tend to misconstrue even the most positive feedback. If organizations want to develop high performers, managers must be equipped to coach and empower them.[27]

Since coaching is so important to us as leaders and to the people we lead, we'll first look at some common problems with coaching. Then we'll present a new, effective way to view this skill, and, finally, explain how truly effective coaching can set your team, and you as a leader, apart in performance.

Why Does Coaching Matter?

The workplace has changed dramatically over the last twenty years and will continue to do so. Technology is removing international borders, leveling the playing field as it transforms it, and even creating entirely new fields. Given this reality, leaders can't rely on static teams with set goals and objectives. Teams are increasingly broader and flatter, more cross-functional and global, and with ever-changing priorities. Leaders now must build for their teams *foundations* of ways to work that will ensure the agility needed for their organizations to survive and thrive. Agility may be *the* workforce objective for the twenty-first century. Ensuring that your team has the feedback it needs to unlock its capability will help the team develop, adapt, and stay ahead of the forces impacting your organization. If they remain stagnant, you may find yourself with a team stuck in the quick-drying cement of complacency. A focus on coaching is foundational to building a high-performing team. As the leader, you must help your team stay connected, relay consistent messages and clear direction, and reinforce the values and culture of your organization. Routine, effective coaching gives you regular time together, allowing you to get and stay on the same page and enabling your team members to move objectives forward. Regular check-ins on values, goals, and desired behaviors reinforce their importance. Connecting on this level consistently and regularly means that other tactical activities will fall into place more easily, enabling agility.

I Have Meetings, Therefore I Coach

Another issue plaguing even solid coaching efforts is the dreaded *routine meeting*: one-on-ones, quarterly reviews, annual reviews, and team meetings are often considered the best way to connect with employees. We need to align: schedule a meeting. We need a strategy refresh: schedule a meeting. We need people to move faster on the change curve: schedule *several* meetings. I need to coach my employees: schedule a meeting. Meetings are an easy "check the box" tactic to keep people in the loop, share work status, and catch issues before they unravel. But don't mistake meeting with your employees about work status for coaching. In fact, in most meetings, anything *but* meaningful sharing is typically happening. People talk, not many listen, and if you watch the nonverbals, you'll realize that meetings can be one of the least effective methods for sharing information, much less coaching.

It's My Job to Change You

Another reason many managers struggle with coaching is that often they confuse it with performance management. Your main job as a leader is to mobilize others toward achieving organizational goals. A simple change in perspective from "help this person change these behaviors or gain these skills" to "connect with people in order to achieve organizational goals together" will naturally lead you to tie your feedback for your employees back to the organization. Ultimately, this is what they really want and need: everyone wants to contribute to a successful team.

A Solution: Connect to Grow

Another reason many managers lack the ability to effectively coach employees is that coaching is the wrong word: consider "connecting" instead. Coaching can create a mind-set of "do unto others," that is, telling people what they need to do and how to be better based on *your* perspective. However, shifting from "coaching" to "connecting" means first establishing trust before providing feedback. Think back to a time you received tough feedback, a time you internalized that feedback and acted on it to make some internal change. Now think about your level of trust with that person: was it someone you knew had your best interests at heart? Feedback on technical or skills opportunities are generally easy to accept, but feedback on softer issues can be tougher to swallow. Most of us will only accept feedback and make the effort to change if we trust the person providing the feedback and can connect the need to change back to our goals or values. Knowing yourself and knowing others gives you the tools to develop meaningful connections, listen, be honest but caring while providing constructive feedback, and watch for and offer the opportunities to help the other person grow. When you're really listening, you can truly understand what matters to your employees. Even when feedback is delivered with trust and caring, the reality is that few people will go through the effort to change without first seeing the "WIIFM," or the "What's in It for Me?" A leader's job, once trust and rapport are built with an employee, is to help each individual find his or her WIIFM for each coaching opportunity. Really listening for what matters to an employee means helping him or her find the alignment between the thing that matters and the change he or she needs to make. Change is hard; it takes energy, and only something that matters is worth the energy that change requires. Add a Connect to Grow approach to your coaching, and your interactions will have the singular, shared goal of achieving organizational objectives, with better performance through meaningful connection. If you can create authentic connections, you can be a good coach.

Author's Note (Christine): Remember that we wrote this book because we had to learn many lessons the hard way, and we wish we'd had a guide to manage our careers more effectively early on. Through trial and error, the one thing that became clear to me, whether managing people or coaching leaders who manage others, is that it takes more time to coach effectively, because everyone is different and needs are always changing. But the act of taking more time to connect is absolutely worth it. It's not about taking more time directing, but rather about taking more time conversing, asking questions, and discussing issues. I once came into a role where I knew specifically what my team's challenges were; I also had a sense of what to do about it fairly quickly. However, I had to pretend that I didn't have that knowledge in order to truly get to know each team member, build each individual's trust through showing my support, and highlight the team's strengths with our client group. Down the road, when difficult conversations needed to happen (and they did), it was much easier. In another case, I spent time with the team to try to understand what we were and could be. Together, we established a vision and a culture of support on our

*team. It wasn't perfect, but over time, issues leveled
out and we achieved much of what we set out to do.*

Connect to Grow: Easy How-To

Much of what you've done for yourself so far in this book will
help you connect, coach, and achieve organizational goals
with your team, which is the real secret behind achieving
organizational results and agility. The following steps can
be helpful as you learn to Connect to Grow; just remember,
keep it simple and informal with the goal to connect and
grow yourself, your team, and the organization together.

1. Know yourself first.

    Sound familiar? That's because knowing yourself is key to
    much of leadership. Walk the talk of developing yourself:
    truly knowing yourself brings the necessary confidence to
    coach others. Have others connected with you authenti-
    cally in the past? What did and didn't work? What have
    you learned from reflecting on the exercises in Knowing
    Yourself and Knowing Others? Share this information as
    appropriate, to build trust and connection as you connect
    with others.

2. Get to know your people.

    Begin connecting by getting to know your team mem-
    bers as individuals: what they value, their skills and de-
    velopment opportunities, what motivates them, how
    they will feel rewarded. Next, share your own goals for
    the organization, and encourage them to share their

ideas about how their values, strengths, and capabilities can contribute to those goals.

3. Learn to listen and observe.

    Look for issues that may be posing obstacles to your team members' achieving the organization's goals, and review the tactics in Knowing Others. Balance constructive feedback with allowing team members to find their own answers to problems, try their own way, and potentially even fail and learn. Watch for signs of awareness of their progress or lack of progress.

4. Establish and develop a Connect to Grow habit.

    On a regular basis (we suggest at least once a week), set aside time to plan your opportunities for that week to provide immediate feedback, ask questions, and offer a connection with each person on your team.

5. Role play.

    Consider including this tool in your Connect to Grow habit, choosing a trusted peer to role play connecting or giving feedback, to gain deeper insight into your style and how your message might be received.

6. Be a learning broker.

    Leverage your formal and informal networks on behalf of your team members by helping them find short-term projects, mentors, or shadowing and other learning opportunities that leverage and grow their skills in line with their personal goals, team goals, and organizational goals. Project examples include project leadership, presentations to senior leadership, market research, plan writing, mentoring, or serving on a board.

If after regular connecting you have team members not carrying forward organization values or goals, then even more connection from you is needed. If the issues continue, at some point you must decide if they belong on the team. You can't afford to have people on your team who won't move the organization forward or who won't embody organizational goals…one toxic person can poison a whole team. While letting someone go is difficult, it's more effective in the long run than having your team's goals held back by the wrong people. This isn't about disagreeing or challenging within the team. Quite the contrary—with a connected team there should be disagreement and freedom to challenge. It's about what people do when they leave the room. Tolerating bad behavior or poor performers is the surest way for you as the leader to remain mediocre, or worse, to fail.

> *Author's Note (Kelly): Early in my career, I had to let someone go who didn't want to adapt to our new team structure. I felt bad for him; his function had moved to company headquarters, and I'd found him a role that I thought he could do and stay on the team. I'd given him*

ample opportunity to learn and adjust and had worked hard to help him make the changes we needed. When it became clear that he didn't really want to be part of the new reality, I realized what I had to do, but it was an agonizing decision: he was a nice guy and well liked by the team. I was still new to the team as its leader and worried what the team's reaction would be to my decision. I dismissed the individual and waited. Several months later, one of his most regular lunch buddies made an indirect comment about how it was best for the team that he was gone. I was stunned but learned a tremendous lesson from it: the team is always impacted by someone who shouldn't be there, even if he's a nice guy and well liked. I've now learned to consider the needs of the whole team as well as the needs of the individual when there's a tough personnel decision to make. While making sure that I'm fair, I also take needed personnel actions quickly, for the sake of the team.

A Final Word: Coaching Models

Since coaching isn't natural to many leaders, many coaching models have been developed to try to help. These models may go in and out of style, depending on who's in charge of development at your organization. It may be most practical to view coaching like any other business process: the more you operate in a regular, consistent, and habitual way, the more effective you'll be. Discovering what works for you is a process. You want to develop a leadership toolbox that fits your style and enables a consistent *habit* of connecting with others. It's important not to get bogged down with any particular process or model, and instead to just take the time to coach. If a coaching model helps you do that, great. If it makes the process awkward or formal, then develop and use your own coaching habit. Doing what works for you is what matters when coaching your team toward accomplishing goals. Remember, it's about connecting, and it's tough to connect if you're not being authentic.

* * *

Additional Resources

Coaching for Performance: GROWing Human Potential and Purpose—the Principles and Practice of Coaching and Leadership, by John Whitmore (Nicholas Brealey, 2009).

Co-Active Coaching: Changing Business, Transforming Lives, by Henry Kimsey-House, Karen Kimsey-House, Phillip Sandahl, and Laura Whitworth (Nicholas Brealey, 2011).

Leadership Companion Exercise: Coaching Others

Assess

1. What formal or informal coaching or mentoring experiences have you had in the past? What worked well? What would have made them more constructive?

   _____

   _____

   _____

2. What natural challenges do you face coaching others? What positive results could you expect by being an effective coach?

   _____

   _____

   _____

3. With the goal of helping grow the organization, what one way could you, and each member of your team, specifically contribute?

   _____

   _____

   _____

Adapt

4. What one step could you take to Connect to Grow together?

_____

_____

_____

Scaling for Organizations

Discuss the questions above as a leadership team; cascade as appropriate through the team.

Leading Complexity

LEADING COMPLEXITY: A PREVIEW

*A leader…is like a shepherd. He stays behind
the flock, letting the most nimble go out ahead,
whereupon the others follow, not realizing that
all along they are being directed from behind.*
—Nelson Mandela

Managing the complexity of larger teams and functions can be deceptively simple. On its surface, leading in a larger role can appear to be nearly the same as managing smaller teams, just with more people. You still need to set vision and inspire; communicate values; establish goals; and get, develop, and keep the right people on the team. But there is one critical adjustment needed: the increase in complexity with more senior roles actually requires a *decrease* in your focus, to deep and wide, on the precious few things that, if done well, will have the most benefit.

Because the demands on you from other organizations' priorities will exponentially increase, delegating that layer of activities on which you used to focus is crucial. You will no longer interact with every person on your team every day, so you must ensure you have strong leaders on your leadership team, as individuals and as a group. Leading larger teams introduces more dependencies with other teams. Knowing yourself and others comes into play even more, as you need to apply the knowledge gained from that self-awareness and your work environment to build key relationships and stay focused on the critical few in the face of many competing priorities and distractions. Just as your larger team will watch carefully for the meaning or symbolism behind your actions, so too will other areas of the organization watch for signs of whether they should collaborate with you and your team. Dependencies between your team and other areas of the organization generally increase along with the size of your team. That means your success now depends not just on your own team, but also on other teams, where you have little or no direct authority and which may have conflicting objectives. You'll also need to start looking up at this point...literally. As your role increases in complexity and size, the external environment becomes more important than previous roles, which may have required you to focus only within your organization.

Two more advanced skills will help as you become a more senior leader with the new dynamic of increased complexity but decreased focus. We start this section with the next evolution in knowing yourself—the concept of emotional intelligence. Daniel Goleman's research provides evidence that the most effective leaders aren't those with the highest intellect or charisma, but instead those with a strong combination of self-awareness of their strengths and opportunities, combined with the self-control to adapt to their situation. Chapter 8 covers the next step in knowing others: influencing. Organizations are increasingly recognizing the value of their leaders' abilities to influence those outside their span of control. The importance of influencing isn't limited to middle- and senior-level leaders, just as leadership isn't limited to certain levels, but it becomes absolutely crucial with larger roles with their broader, more complex scopes and increasing dependencies. Finally, before moving to the last section of Strategic Leadership, we felt it important to address and provide guidance on career transitions, which we do in chapter 9. Change—whether planned or unplanned—is inevitable in your career. Applying the concepts and assessments you've learned up to this point can help you navigate those transitions more smoothly.

It's important to understand how managing the complexity of a large team is different from managing a smaller one. You'll be responsible for setting the tone and getting things done with and through other teams where you don't have direct authority. You'll need to limit the distractions created by others' priorities for you and your team in order to keep from losing focus. Making the effort to master this step change not only prepares you for a larger role, it could also help you to make a bigger impact on your organization.

CHAPTER 7

Emotional Intelligence

*Emotions are contagious. We've all known
it experientially. You know after you have
a really fun coffee with a friend, you feel
good. When you have a rude clerk in a
store, you walk away feeling bad.*

–DANIEL GOLEMAN

EI, Not IQ

When we think of what makes a truly good leader, we don't usually point to intellectual qualities, such as a high IQ or GPA, an advanced education, or strong analytical ability. Instead, we think of qualities such as integrity, empathy, and the ability to inspire. We have a tendency to believe that these qualities are inherent, much like traditional intelligence: you're either born with these skills or you aren't. Research on emotional intelligence shows that these skills actually *can* be practiced and learned.

Emotional intelligence builds on the awareness gained earlier in Knowing Yourself and Knowing Others. We now turn that basic awareness into action, with a more advanced focus on noticing and regulating emotions in ourselves and in others. The exercises at the beginning of the book helped build knowledge, awareness, and habits, but the ability to adapt where needed is *the* prize: emotional intelligence aims to take knowledge of self and apply it to emotions and behavior, a critical step toward developing the skill of adaptability while remaining true to yourself.

We shouldn't just adapt to everything that comes along; rather, we should be selective and adapt only when doing so aligns to our goals or builds our skills or our reputation. The times we experience the greatest challenges—when we're really put to the test—are often times that require integrity, or staying true to ourselves. You'll be best able to demonstrate integrity if you can identify emotional triggers in yourself and others, and thoughtfully choose a reaction in line with your core values. That—practiced well and consistently—is the heart of emotional intelligence.

Bear with Us: An Emotional Intelligence (EI) Refresher

Many of you have heard of EI, but we want to align through a quick refresher, as the term can be misunderstood. Up until about twenty years ago, the concept of intelligence was limited to scholastic achievement, test scores, and IQs. Then, Daniel Goleman challenged traditional assumptions about intelligence with his bestselling 1998 book *Emotional Intelligence: Why It Can Matter More Than IQ.*

> The rules for work are changing. We're being judged by a new yardstick: not just by how smart we are, or by our training and expertise, but also by how well we handle ourselves and each other. This yardstick is increasingly applied in choosing who'll be hired and who won't, who'll be let go and who retained, who passed over and who promoted. The new rules predict who's most likely to become a star performer, and who's most prone to derailing.[28]

Think about that last statement: "most prone to derailing." Right there is where knowing yourself and others and adaptability meet—where awareness meets practice. Without both awareness and practice, those blind spots become derailers.

According to Goleman, there are five components of EI at work: self-awareness, self-regulation, motivation, empathy, and social skill.[29]

EI Components	Definition	Hallmarks
Self-awareness	Knowing one's emotions, strengths, weaknesses, drives, values, and goals—and their impact on others	▪ Self-confidence ▪ Realistic self-assessment ▪ Self-deprecating sense of humor ▪ Thirst for constructive criticism
Self-regulation	Controlling or redirecting disruptive emotions and impulses	▪ Trustworthiness ▪ Integrity ▪ Comfort with ambiguity and change
Motivation	Being driven to achieve for the sake of achievement	▪ A passion for the work itself and for new challenges ▪ Unflagging energy to improve ▪ Optimism in the face of failure
Empathy	Considering others' feelings, especially when making decisions	▪ Expertise in attracting and retaining talent ▪ Ability to develop others ▪ Sensitivity to cross-cultural differences

Social skill	Managing relationships to move people in desired directions	<ul><li>Effectiveness in leading change</li><li>Persuasiveness</li><li>Extensive networking</li><li>Expertise in building and leading teams[30]</li></ul>

Further, Goleman describes competencies as falling into three core domains: technical skills (for example, software programming), cognitive abilities (for example, analytical reasoning), and abilities in the EI range (such as customer service or conflict management abilities). These EI-based competencies combine both cognitive and emotional skills and are distinguished from purely cognitive abilities, such as IQ, and from technical skills, which have no such emotional component.[31] Goleman says,

> When I analyzed all this data, I found dramatic results. To be sure, intellect was a driver of outstanding performance. Cognitive skills such as big-picture thinking and long-term vision were particularly important. But when I calculated the ratio of technical skills, IQ, and Emotional Intelligence as ingredients of excellent performance, Emotional Intelligence proved to be twice as important as the others for jobs at all levels.[32]

This research is consistent with our belief and our passion that anyone can lead at any level. You could argue that someone described as emotionally intelligent is simply someone who has a deep knowledge of self and others and who adapts easily, keeping core values intact. By practicing the skills and exercises in Knowing Yourself and Knowing Others, you're developing the habit of self-reflection, which is foundational for developing emotional intelligence.

Where the Lack of EI Tends to Show Up

Personal conflicts can wreak havoc in the workplace, leading to misunderstandings, work breakdowns, and petty competitiveness that can border on the ridiculous. Unnecessary conflicts can arise because people take things personally, instead of being grounded in self-awareness and realizing that there's a more truthful and productive way to view conflict: to see it as information about some*thing* and not some*one* (namely, you).

When you're practicing EI—recognizing others' emotions, having empathy, and regulating your emotions—you recognize that situations are not about you, but rather about a combination of many factors, most of which you aren't privy to. You can see conflict for what it really is: information being communicated versus a personal rejection. With an information-gathering mind-set, you can ask questions, confirm what you've heard, and offer other possibilities. With an "I'm being rejected" perspective, there's no problem solving to be done, only a dead-end pity party, complete with a gripe session with a co-worker, and an ongoing conflict. Catherine Chen, PhD, said in her *Huffington Post* article, "Effective Leadership: How to Not Take Things Personally," that a key way of overcoming this taking-it-personally hurdle is by seeking to understand the other's perspective.

> Defensiveness rises from assumptions about the unknown that are believed to be true. Before jumping to conclusions, ask questions to clarify where others' actions, inactions, or inquiries are coming from. If you really put an effort into this, you'll often find that it has nothing to do with you. Maybe the boss wants more sales or to conserve resources. Or, there is a series of personal events that you didn't know about that led up to them seemingly taking it out on you. Or, your colleague was trained to think a certain way, and so it's hard for them to accept your point of view. By understanding their perspective, you'll realize that things don't happen to you, they just happen.[33]

By taking *you* out of the equation and listening with empathy, conflict can be minimized and more quickly resolved. You are the leader; people are watching you, and your brand will get a boost if you can resolve conflict quickly and constructively. Every time you act in this way, you reinforce the skill of self-restraint and can move things forward. Every time you take things personally, you hold yourself back. The simple act of not taking things personally opens the door to the critical self-regulation component of EI. Do that, and you've crossed a major threshold toward mastering EI.

"Why does self-regulation matter so much for leaders?" Goleman asks.

First of all, people who are in control of their feelings and impulses—that is, people who are reasonable—are able to create an environment of trust and fairness. In such an environment, politics and infighting are sharply reduced, and productivity is high. Talented people flock to the organization and aren't tempted to leave. And self-regulation has a trickle-down effect. No one wants to be known as a hothead when the boss is known for her calm approach. Fewer bad moods at the top mean fewer throughout the organization.[34]

Author's Note (Christine): The biggest personal lessons I learned about emotional intelligence are when I've allowed people to get to me, particularly when working with jerks. I have a separate being inside who only shows up when someone displays disrespectful, bullying, patronizing, dismissive, or insulting behavior toward me or toward others. I've learned over the years that I won't ever master dealing with jerks, but I've changed how I deal with them. I don't take their behavior personally anymore, which gives me the courage to confront them. While it takes a lot of planning and energy, I now let them know that I won't tolerate that behavior. But I have to be careful not to swing the pendulum the other way, from doing nothing to tackling all jerks. I'm on a journey to determine which jerks are worth the EI effort and subsequent candid conversation, and which ones are best ignored. Some relationships are more important than others, but it's important not to tolerate repeated, poor behavior toward you or others.

Make an Impact Right Now: Five Quick, Easy Steps for EI Anytime, Anyplace

Resolve conflict and find common ground by replacing an emotional reaction to conflicts with these five steps:

1. Recognize people's emotions.
2. Empathize: realize how strongly they must actually feel and how hard this is for them.
3. Take a deep breath.
4. Recognize your own emotions and reactions to this situation, and name them. For example: *Anger, Resentment, Humiliation,* or *Rejection.*
5. Mentally send the emotion away and refocus, starting with step 1.

The Hidden Prize of Empathy in Practice: Strong Relationships

Empathy goes a long way to defining our character and our brand. Empathy is often misconstrued as pity, taking on someone else's emotions, or giving away power. But as defined in Goleman's EI model, it's simply about acknowledging the emotions of others, if only for the sake of moving forward. Our effort to understand others' needs and concerns builds trust and long-term credibility. Expressing that empathy builds relationships. It also creates followers, attracts and retains talented people, and strengthens your brand. Goleman says,

> Consider the challenge of leading a team. As anyone who has ever been a part of one can attest, teams are cauldrons of bubbling emotions. They are often charged with reaching a consensus—which is hard enough with two people and much more difficult as the numbers increase. Even in groups with as few as four or five members, alliances form and clashing agendas get set. A team's leader must be able to sense and understand the viewpoints of everyone around the table.[35]

Work gets done through others, and those others want to be heard. Proceeding with the assumption that we don't have all the answers, and engaging people thoughtfully because we need them, is empathy in action, and the resulting discussion and follow-through builds trust. The ability to build rapport quickly and to find common ground is necessary for effectively leading large-scale organizations.

Empathy is also helpful when leading your organization through large-scale change. No matter how much you prepare or communicate, some people just aren't going to see your side of things. Instead of focusing on what others aren't doing, focus instead on what you're doing. The true leader's path to adaptability comes from embracing those you don't agree with and believing there's something to learn from them, without spending too much time on them.

Other Benefits of EI

Finally, EI allows you to move through failure gracefully. This isn't only good for you, it's also critical for the people you lead: if you remain stuck, they remain stuck.

Emotional intelligence can help you discover the learning opportunity in failure, by stepping back from taking it personally, regulating your emotional response to the situation, and quickly and objectively admitting to missteps. This can keep you from derailing, quickly shifting the focus forward to possibilities, to how to make it better.

Think about those things that drive you crazy, that eat at you. Emotional intelligence is about being aware of those emotions, about looking at them and choosing your reaction, a reaction that's aligned with your values and your brand. Move *toward* these items with your EI understanding in hand: acknowledge how you're affected, choose to learn from the situation, and remain open through listening to others.

Companies still have a long way to go in rewarding and advancing people with these qualities. How often do you still hear of, or know, individuals who advanced into leadership only because they excelled as individual contributors? But a momentum is developing. Large shifts in skill needs, such as change catalysts and leveraging diversity[36] have resulted from unending market and process shifts in companies, not to mention the rapid pace of globalization.[37] According to Goleman's research, with one exception—"big-picture" thinking—intellectual or technical abilities play no real role in leadership success: "Emotional competence made the crucial difference between mediocre leaders and the best. On average, close to 90 percent of their success in leadership was attributable to emotional intelligence."[38] Emotional intelligence can be key to your success as a leader as well.

∗   ∗   ∗

Additional Resources

Emotional Intelligence: Why It Can Matter More Than IQ, by Daniel Goleman (Bantam Books, 2005).

Leadership Companion Exercise: Emotional Intelligence

Assess

1. What issues do you currently struggle with within the five areas of EI (self-awareness, self-regulation, motivation, empathy, and social skill)? How do they hold you back?

   _____

   _____

   _____

2. How are these challenges consistent with the insights you've gained in the Knowing Yourself and Knowing Others exercises?

   _____

   _____

   _____

3. What one or two things do you need your entire team focused on to be successful? What EI areas are hampering that focus today?

   _____

   _____

   _____

Adapt

4. Pick the challenge of EI from number 1 that you most struggle with. Put a daily reminder on your calendar for one month to monitor and adapt your typical reactions to those triggers.

5. Incorporate the EI information you've identified above into the mini-communication plan you developed in the chapter 3 Leadership Companion exercise.

Scaling for Organizations

Discuss with your team the areas of EI that may be hampering the team's success toward a key goal; brainstorm ways to overcome the hurdles.

CHAPTER 8

Influencing Others

The key to successful leadership
today is influence, not authority.

—KEN BLANCHARD

Why Influence?

Influencing is crucial in larger leadership roles, but even individual contributors early in their careers will accomplish more, and be thought of as leaders earlier, if they can effectively influence. Many think of influencing as difficult, probably because not all leaders are good at it. But influencing can be understood and learned. Influential leadership is critical when you have:

- A need for a broader span of influence, beyond your immediate team to other areas across the organization
- Less control over a widening group of people critical to your work

- Competing priorities with other teams
- A need to influence more senior-level leaders
- A need to move the organization to change

Let's say your organization is falling behind. Customers and suppliers have been giving signs for years that change is needed in your organization. Initiatives were started and progress was made, but it's becoming more evident that external change has outpaced your ability to respond. Meanwhile, things feel normal internally. There's no burning platform. If you asked most employees, they would say things are fine. You have mass complacency. If you're a leader faced with this situation, or any number of other scenarios in which change is needed, the skill in your arsenal to get people aligned and motivated to change is influence. Your ability to influence is an indication that you're moving further along the continuum of true leadership.

Influence isn't necessarily about getting what you want. Influence has to come from a genuine place, one that's in line with the organization's goals, is best for the customer or the team, or inherently improves the organization. Influencing for self-benefit will be identified quickly as manipulation. Organizations often reward this "me first" behavior without even realizing it, and spiral down with resulting problems such as turnover, poor results, and low engagement. You don't have to be that kind of leader. Influence is about getting things done with others, meeting beneficial goals in a highly complex environment. It isn't about being charismatic, charming, manipulative, or any of the other attributes sometimes associated with influence. It's never about becoming something or someone else. It's about knowing yourself, knowing others, and having tools you can apply that are consistent with your values to get things done for the good of the organization.

Influencing Versus Directing

Successful influencing depends not only on the approach of the leader but also on the response of recipients. People who influence well generally receive respect, trust, and followership. This can be true of directing, too. But directing can sometimes cause resentment. Influencing takes more time; its key traits are a genuine interest in and advocacy of others and working toward a common goal. Conversely, directing is simply that: directing others to do something. Leading only by directing is exhausting, because no one grows, and as the environment shifts and demands grow more sophisticated, the need to direct only grows. People aren't thinking when they're being told what to do. Influencers create thinking organizations. Empowered thinkers trust leadership, adapt quickly, and grow. Directive styles create the opposite effect of complacency. However, both directing and influence have their places. There are times when directing is the most appropriate action, particularly when the task is routine, when time is short, or during a crisis. Often, one style is more natural to leaders and they have to sharpen the other. For many leaders, directing is the natural style, since that's how they first became the boss.

One perceived downside of influencing successfully is that it may seem that it takes longer than directing. In the short run, directing is faster. In the end, however, directing can take longer if the task needs buy-in for it to "stick" with those being directed. In making big or meaningful change, you have a choice: you can either mandate quick change and potentially suffer lost time, productivity, and angst on the back end, or you can work to engage people and bring them along for a more positive overall experience, building the trust to speed future transitions. For big changes, both directing and influencing will likely take about the same amount of time overall—influencing just shifts the effort to the front end versus cleaning up afterward. It takes patience to bring people along, but they'll better support the change. It will always seem there isn't enough time to engage important stakeholders and allow for support to unfold. You do need to strike a balance between a practical "now" and "too long" for change. For example, build in time to shop around your concepts, but offer specific dates and needs for when action will be taken. Actively listen and be flexible when legitimate concerns could affect the outcome.

Influencing to change is more effective in the long term because of gains made beyond the task, including building trust, leading to improved retention. Most importantly, the goodwill from influencing to change carries over to future changes you need to make, encouraging others to want to follow you the next time. Most people respond positively in the long term to being brought along with change versus just being told to "go there." A directing leader may wonder where all the good people went during and after the change and may face greater opposition during future changes.

Types of Influence

Types of influence are closely aligned to the types of authority outlined in chapter 4: Leadership Fundamentals and Authority. Positional influence refers to using your position of authority to influence change, or, put simply, "I'm your boss/project leader/ vice president, so do this because I said so." Positional influence works in the short term and for specific tasks, but isn't the most effective for large-scale change. The most effective use for positional influence is when teams are at a crossroads and it's time for decisiveness. Sometimes leaders do have to make a call, but ideally only after all other attempts to gain traction have been exhausted. Another appropriate use of positional influence is when the stakes of a decision are high. Since the buck stops at the top, it's appropriate for the boss to make the tough decisions.

But it's personal authority, not positional, that is most effective for influencing. Leveraging as many of the forms of personal authority as possible gives you the best chance at pulling the right lever for each given situation or stakeholder. Influence can come from having deep industry knowledge or expertise, as people may respond more favorably to directions given by an expert. Relational influence, or the ability to influence through relationships, is the most valuable skill to master because it applies broadly, in any situation. While the complexity of exercising influence throughout your career increases along with the complexity of your role, the tactics are surprisingly similar no matter where you are in your career. The concepts covered in the chapters "Knowing Yourself," "Knowing Others," and "Emotional Intelligence" will help you develop influencing skills. If you've identified and are living your core values, and you know how you show up to others, you have a great start on influencing.

Effective influencing requires both planning and listening. Bring others along via the art of getting buy-in. You can employ basic change management principles such as developing a stakeholder analysis and communication plan. You can also build a relationship plan by identifying those in positions of power and decision makers who are key to your and the team's success. Remember, you need to build partners before you need them, so assess your level of partnership with them today and assess what you need to do to improve the relationship. Identify goals for your alliances and plan actions to build the relationships. This could include people critical to your career success or those who are key to achieving your team's goals. Listen, really listen, to other stakeholders to identify their goals and concerns. Find and focus on a common purpose, recognizing that most disagreement occurs over the "how" rather than the "what." Every situation is different. Just being conscious of the need to approach every stakeholder and solicit input appropriately is the first step to aligning and getting things done together.

Author's Note (Christine): I had the good fortune of working with an insightful leader during an acquisition integration. He was a true partner, and we shared many similar perspectives. That said, the boiling cauldron of employee and group dynamics while integrating two organizations was exhausting, and the workload was massive. I became more courageous and, necessarily, more blunt to just get through all that we had to get done. This leader gave me feedback that my insights were spot on, but that I was three meetings ahead of everybody else. I needed to meet them where they were and bring them along. I've always felt this need, but was never able to articulate it myself, which is why feedback from others is so important. I often feel like I see things others don't or won't, and that sometimes they're a year away from being ready to acknowledge something that I can see that is really holding them back. With a personal tendency to want immediate results, and a strong sense of courage that I've developed over the years, how can I be courageous and still bring people along? And when is it important to just go with courage and not worry about the impact? When it's simply the right thing to do—honesty, integrity, treating people respectfully—I don't wish to learn to influence. Frankly, the world could use a little more courage in these areas. For other, noncore values, I've learned to get to know as many people as possible in the organization through any work-related excuse I can find, and then explore the tough topics within that context. I've learned to listen, take notes, get their perspective, and confirm that we share the value in question...that's the first step. Then in the context of other meetings or discussions, I can bring up the value area that needs improvement. I keep bringing it up in a variety of different ways and with different people. Eventually, you have to be willing to put something out there, but by then it will be expected. In one case, it took me an entire year to explore shared goals on a team. It was inconceivable the first time I brought it up, but with diligent follow through, eventually my suggestions were accepted and executed.

What about Getting Credit?

There's a potential, though limited, downside to successful influencing, and that concerns getting credit. Often those who effectively influence find that others come to their conclusion magically "on their own"—sometimes quickly, sometimes much delayed. Because an influencer presents options and empathizes with others' needs and concerns, it's often squishy who gets credit for landing in the right place. This can drive a controlling person crazy. At most, it merely irritates an influencer, because it's the accomplishment, and not who accomplished it, that matters most. They also rightfully presume that those "in the know" likely realize who conceived the idea in the first place, even if they don't directly say so. Influencing requires the maturity to accept that outcome, which enables even more influencing. Yet while effective influencers often find that they don't always immediately "get credit" for an outcome, even when deserved, the relationships they build and the results they achieve with others often leaves others wanting to work with them again. In short, they're seen as effective leaders, even if specific results don't fully stick to them. Instead, over time it's recognized that they simply get more done, and done the right way.

Developing Your Leadership Brand

While your focus needs to be on what's best for the organization, that doesn't mean you don't personally benefit by influencing. We all have a leadership brand, whether we've ever thought about it or not. Do you know what yours is? From the first day on any job, you begin to leave an impression on others. The simplest way to think about your brand is to think about your reputation. Your brand will impact your effectiveness as a leader, especially in new settings or with new team members, and will either help or hurt you.

Author's Note (Christine): My profound experience with leadership brand happened early in my career. I was a project manager at a small communications firm and was a Fast Company magazine subscriber. At the time, Fast Company was a cutting-edge business periodical that really resonated with me. Their publication of Tom Peters's article "The Brand Called You" was transformative.[39] I carried that magazine around with me for months and kept it on my office shelf for years. It was the first time that I viewed myself as someone with something unique to offer...that I had a history, skills, and future different from everybody else, and that I should actively tell that story. Previously, I'd viewed myself as an employee lucky to have any job, having graduated from college in the early 1990s recession. I can't say this mind-set change transformed my life, but it was always in the back of my mind when I sought out new opportunities, looked at career changes, and even made the decision to pursue my MBA—a less likely path for a communications person, but one that I pursued partially because of what I wanted to be known for by clients: a quick-study, pragmatic, smart, business-minded consultant capable of different roles supporting many industries.

Effective leaders actively monitor and nurture their leadership brand, aware that it greatly affects their ability to influence others. When you approach others needing their help, people will refer to their prior experiences with you (one aspect of your brand) as they decide whether to help you, particularly if it's difficult to do so. Have you helped them in the past? Did you approach them cooperatively in prior experiences, looking for win-win outcomes, or at least outcomes that were clearly best for the organization? Or do you have a track record of running over everyone in your way to achieve your agenda? People who don't know you will rely partly on what they see from you, but they're also likely to rely just as heavily on what they hear from those who've worked with you.

Do you know what your leadership brand is? What have others complimented you on or complained about? What has your boss told you in your performance evaluations? What themes have you heard in 360 feedback evaluations? All of these, especially in combination, are strong indicators of your brand.

Proactively managing your leadership brand is not complicated. Knowing what it is today versus what you want it to be is by far the most important step. A *Harvard Business Review* article about the topic suggests getting feedback on your brand, but also that you complete the sentence, "I wish to be known for _____."[40] Then, you can begin planning actions to reinforce where it's already strong and consistent with what you want to be known for, and build up where you have opportunities or gaps. Reflecting on how effective you are at influencing others is another, though less direct, way of assessing the effectiveness of your brand.

As you can see, we're building on concepts throughout the book: knowing yourself, knowing others, and emotional intelligence position you to influence, build trust, and create an intentional brand. Having a positive brand means others will be more likely to want to follow you. Influencing techniques work to align with others on mutual objectives. This builds your brand and brings others along, getting things done through others—not because they have to, but because they want to. Getting alignment with others to get things done is the hallmark of influencing and is required for fully effective leadership, particularly at more senior levels.

* * *

Additional Resources

How to Win Friends & Influence People, by Dale Carnegie (Pocket Books, 1998).

Silent Influencing: Employing Powerful Techniques for Influence and Leadership, by Michael Nir, Philip Pekar, and Chen Nir (CreateSpace Independent Publishing Platform, 2012).

Compelling People: The Hidden Qualities That Make Us Influential, by John Neffinger and Matthew Kohut (Plume, 2014).

Leadership Companion Exercise: Influencing Others

Assess

1. Think of a change you've gone through where business or service disruptions were minimal and morale was stable. What limited the impact of the change?

   _____

   _____

   _____

2. Conversely, think of a change that saw tremendous interruptions and led to low morale. What increased the negative impact of the change?

   _____

   _____

   _____

Adapt

3. Think of someone with influencing skills that you admire. What can you learn from his or her style that applies naturally to your own? What adjustments may you need to make to fit your style?

   _____

   _____

   _____

4. Ask three trusted people, "What do you think is my brand (i.e., what do you think of first when you think of me)?" Reflect on what is and is not a surprise. What adjustments, if any, do you want to make given the results?

_____

_____

_____

Scaling for Organizations

Bring a team through the influencing exercises above and the brand feedback question. What did team members learn about themselves? Are there themes on the team?

_____

_____

_____

CHAPTER 9

A How-To: The Five Most Common Career Changes

*Twenty years from now you will be more
disappointed by the things that you
didn't do than by the ones you did do,
so throw off the bowlines, sail away from
safe harbor, catch the trade winds in
your sails. Explore. Dream. Discover.*

–MARK TWAIN

n the past, careers began after graduation from college, by finding a job in our field. People stayed in their first industry, and often even that first company, throughout their careers. Corporate environments were more predictable, with tried and true career paths. But for some time now, we've been in a workforce at the mercy of external factors: the global economy, short-term shareholder goals, unprecedented economic swings, and technology advances. It's common now to face ongoing uncertainty, whatever your chosen field. Change is increasingly inevitable…you can either choose the change or let it happen to you. While most of us end up with a mix of both, most of us prefer driving the change that will happen to us. The implications to leaders of continuous, often profound, change are equally important: leading people with less traditional backgrounds and experiences requires a progressive view that values core skills and diverse experiences over "institutional" knowledge. Leading others through change also requires the ability to build trust to help them stay engaged through uncertainty.

Reduce the Stress of Change

Career changes can be exciting, but they're also usually stressful. Understanding the risks and opportunities in transitions, no matter the change, will help you move through any event—whether planned or unexpected—more purposefully. Here's a checklist to help you manage through transitions commonly experienced in careers and in life:

- ☐ Get grounded in you. Complete, reread, or update the exercises in this book.
- ☐ Stay connected to others; remain a part of a community that has meaning to you.
- ☐ Reach out to others; help others in need.
- ☐ Ask yourself first thing each morning, "What do I need to do *today* to further my goal of _____ (finding a job, deciding what to do next, changing careers, etc.)?"

☐ Have a plan for when things don't go as planned in the transition. Examples: ask a friend or associate to keep you accountable, reach out to someone for help and advice.

☐ Plot out a daily routine to help you manage through the transition (e.g., meditation, visualization, yoga, exercise, or other activities built into your routine).

☐ Monitor your self-talk and limiting beliefs. Reword from "This is too hard / I can't do this / Why won't X happen" to "Everything that happens today is furthering my growth and development toward X."

☐ Establish a mantra you can use when your mind starts focusing on a worst-case scenario. Replace it with a simple, calming statement, for example: "Expect great things / I will land in a better place no matter what / Stay the course / I am achieving my goals."

Moving effectively and confidently through transitions means knowing yourself and establishing a daily or weekly habit of small actions to stay on track. Embracing the inevitable ambiguity about each unique step in your journey is possible with this basic preparation.

The Most Important Way to Be Prepared for Change

This may seem off topic, but it's nearly impossible to address the crossroads you'll frequently experience in your career without addressing this obvious reality: in addition to the tools in this book, economic freedom is the single most important thing that enables you to express your passion and do what you're good at.

Not being able to act in line with your values or make choices that move you toward a new goal are easily excused away by that very real need for a paycheck, especially if you have a pension or stock plan through your employer. The term "golden handcuffs" isn't some clever term reserved for big executive pay packages; corporations are filled with millions of people who long ago gave up trying to do the right thing, push change, or do work in line with their values, in exchange for a future payout. Although it can be tough to admit, we clearly can be bought. If you love your job and wouldn't change a thing, then it's not an issue. But many stay in jobs for the money or retirement fund, leading to mass complacency, which doesn't help them or their employers.

Even the most basic financial freedom could mean a profound level of choice for you: for example, having an employable spouse, living on one income, and having enough savings to pay fixed expenses for six months. Do what you have to do now to increase your financial freedom. That may take years, but think of it as taking a short-term versus a long-term mortgage: you're paying more principal in the short term, paying off the loan more quickly and saving thousands of dollars in interest payments.

The Five Most Common Career Events You'll Encounter

Changing Jobs

Changing jobs is something nearly everyone does, but not always for the right reasons. Understanding your true motivations and goals will help make potential job changes more successful. According to the Department of Labor, "by the age of 42, you will probably already have had about ten jobs."[41]

Most people change jobs to leave a situation due to tangible dissatisfactions.

Following are the top reasons people change jobs, according to Career Advice Online:[42]

1. Frustration and disillusionment; not using best abilities in current job
2. Redundancy or business closure
3. Working in a declining industry
4. Realignment of personal/spiritual values, midlife reevaluation
5. Dislike of the organizational culture
6. Money

Further, "Research suggests that up to 80 percent of people are not happy in their current job, and the main reason for this is a mismatch between what they are good at and what they are currently doing."[43]

New opportunities often eliminate one or two of your issues with your old job, but they also likely present a whole new set of unexpected challenges, thus potentially putting you back in the same place, just exchanging a set of old problems for a set of new ones. There are dozens of other factors to consider and assumptions to check to ensure you don't end up in the same situation, just in a different setting. Most importantly, through knowing yourself and the other tools in this book, you won't need to run from something, but, rather, can proactively run to something that fits your values and goals. Even if leaving your job isn't an immediate option, once you have a clear picture of yourself and your way with others, you can be at peace with reframing and accepting things that are mere nuisances versus real issues.

Whatever your reasons for wanting to change jobs, be sure you fully understand the "why" for your desire to change. If it's truly external to you—the culture is rotten or the boss stinks— then there's good reason to change. But if you're kidding your-self, and the real reasons are internal, you may find that you take your problems with you. You'll be dealing with the same issues, just with different scenery.

Changing Careers

When you completed the Knowing Yourself exercises, did you discover a big gap between what you're doing today and what matters to you? There are almost as many books about changing careers as there are about leadership, so the attempt here is to provide the basics of any successful career change.

Changing careers is different from changing jobs. For the sake of simplicity, we'll consider a job change as moving from one job to another in a similar industry or function, for example, Sales Job X to Sales Job Y. A career change would be moving from one profession to another, for example: leaving a corporate job to start your own business; going from communications manager to business HR manager; or moving from project manager to Pilates instructor. Statistics as to how many people change careers are conflicting; because of the difficulty in defining career change, the Bureau of Labor Statistics doesn't even try to capture the data. However, since there's a possibility that you may want to change careers at some point, it's worth some time exploring it.

The reasons for career change are very similar to those of a job change, just more extreme. Here are some suggested steps for making an effective career change:

Know Why You're Changing

People will wrestle with such a change for months, even years, and rightfully so: you're likely starting over, or almost starting over, in a brand-new type of job you're unfamiliar with; you need to build new network contacts; and likely you're feeling the impact on your finances and your family. The fear of the unknown or of making the wrong decision for the wrong reasons is scary enough that many people only dream of changing their careers. Maybe you've tried different jobs in your line of work but meet the same dissatisfaction, or maybe you're one of the lucky few who've known what you want to be doing all along. You may know that something needs to change: you don't feel that you fit, and you dislike many aspects of your work. Other reasons for a change might include a lack of career mobility (career or industry are stagnated); having always had a passion for something and you're finally ready to commit to it; or preparing yourself for a broader role in the future (e.g., marketing to sales, finance to HR, etc.).

Build the Bridge with Current Skills

Some people in your new industry will struggle to get past that you didn't grow up in that industry. One of the best ways to get people past that is to identify your current skills that are transferrable to your next career, and specifically how they will transfer, with real live examples. Help others see the ways in which you've already been doing the core of the new career all along, especially if you can point to a key skill that you possess which fills a gap in the new profession. You've also done your homework, so you know enough about the new work environment to give examples of how your skills are used in the most critical of situations in your new career. At every turn, your job is to confidently communicate possibilities.

Network is King

Your network is the most critical career asset you have, and having a strong one becomes mandatory during a career change. If you're meeting with people whom you need to convince that you can do the new job—even though you haven't done it yet—doing your homework and identifying skills that transfer will lower that barrier. However, the best way to land a job in your chosen field is to be referred by someone who can speak to your "core" skills, such as integrity, self-motivation, being enterprising, and so on. People are always going to be more positive about taking a chance with someone who gets a thumbs-up from someone they respect. Also, meet with as many people as possible in your future career. Come prepared with as much knowledge about their jobs as you can, a succinct "elevator speech" about why you seek to change careers to *this* particular career, and then start peppering them with questions. What do you love about your career? What are your frustrations? What's the career path or opportunity for advancement? What is your background? How did you choose this field? Describe your past jobs. What does it take to be successful in this career? What advice would you have for someone like me trying to break into this field? What do you know now that you wish you'd known when you first started out? Offer gratitude for the information and offer to stay in touch regarding your progress. That's it. Don't ask if they have openings now or will later. Resist the temptation to overtly prove your capabilities. The goals for informational interviews are to get "real world" information and establish rapport.

Be Passionate

Instead of "changing careers," you may as well call it "VP of Sales for Me." Selling yourself to someone in a totally different field is akin to getting someone to buy something they don't want or need. You have to be passionate about this career and what impact you can have in it. If you're finding yourself manufacturing this passion, you should ask yourself if it's really the right move, because your interviewees will see it right away.

Going Back to School

According to the Pew Research Center, "63 percent of those who are working (or 36 percent of all adults) are what we call 'professional learners'—that is, they have taken a course or gotten additional training in the past 12 months to improve their job skills or expertise connected to career advancement."[44] The most common reasons people go back to school are to gain skills to move into a new industry or profession, or to keep up with the increasing qualifications for higher-level jobs. For example, a growing number of corporations today prefer candidates with MBAs for management positions. Some also add a more technical undergraduate degree like engineering or IT to their MBA to expand their opportunities. Others are going back to school because they can't find jobs. And some go back to school for simpler reasons: the hope of better career opportunities and more money.

There's debate over whether it's worth the cost to return to school for midcareer employees. Depending on where you are in your career and the long-term cost of both the education and any forgone wages while you're in school, going back to school may not be the best financial decision. If you're taking out student loans, Mark Kantrowitz, publisher of the college-information websites Fastweb.com and Finaid.org, offered this rule of thumb: Don't borrow more than you can pay in ten years or by the time you retire, whichever comes first. Student loan payments should be ten percent or less of your gross income.[45]

A good financial option can be demonstrating to your employer how further education will advance your current skills and meet their needs for talent, in the hopes that they will pay for it. While this can be a challenging commitment—attending school while you're working—it's a great option for paying for it and then using the knowledge and skills you're gaining "just in time." If you're planning to go back to school as part of an overall career change strategy, make sure you explore that new career with people doing that work today. It's possible that you already have enough transferrable skills to make an entry into that career without the cost and time burden of additional education.

Getting Laid Off

This is by far the hardest of the change topics for an obvious reason: all of the others involve a choice. With a layoff, change is forced upon you. Feelings of panic, fear, and questioning of one's self-worth are normal. However, the best way to weather being laid off is to pretend that you've been laid off, even before you are. View it a bit like preventative care or taking out an insurance plan for an important asset—in this case your career. Do all of the things that career experts say to do once you've been laid off, the most important being maintaining your network, knowing yourself, knowing others, and becoming more financially secure. Find ways to manage the stress and stay positive, complete the exercises in Knowing Yourself to get some direction, and work your network. Remember, you are unique, and you have something of unique value to bring somewhere new.

Leaving the Workplace to Be a Caregiver

According to *The Solutions Journal* article "A Revolutionary Change: Making the Workplace More Flexible," caregivers of children or elderly parents face unprecedented challenges in the worldwide workforce today. For the first time in our history, approximately four out of every ten mothers in the United States are primary breadwinners, and almost two-thirds are breadwinners or co-breadwinners.[46] This dynamic has transformed American marriages and families, with couples working more collaboratively in order to juggle careers and caregiving, creating the need for a paradigm shift in how work is done. Despite these demographic shifts, the current model of work is still based in part on an outdated 1950s view, when middle-class families had a single breadwinner and women stayed at home to care for children."[47]

Today, women (and men, too) are leaving the workplace to care for children. This can be a daunting decision or an easy one: each person and situation is different, and there's no right or wrong choice. Often the decision to leave the workplace begins as a financial one, but there are long-term effects to consider as well. Removing an entire income from the family has a tangible impact: it's something you can easily plan in terms of affordability, but other, more unpredictable financial considerations include the impact on future savings, the potential for unexpected costs, and the employment status of the wage earner. Leaving the workplace can free up the working partner to take on more responsibility, enabling promotions and growth opportunities. However, the impact of the single earner losing his or her job becomes a significant risk.

There's also the subtler impact of the mental health of the partner who leaves the workplace, and the increased stress left on the primary earner. Both partners need to take concurrent but somewhat different steps to ensure maximum well-being. For example, both will need a strong support network. The working partner may find his or her network through a regular workout routine or outings with friends. For the caregiver, maintaining connections with former colleagues can be critical. Continue reading books that pertain to your career or interests. Consider trading "mom/dad club" time for a sitter and lunch with a professional colleague. It also doesn't hurt to try doing something you can position professionally if and when you decide to reenter the workplace, such as volunteering your skills to boards, churches, or other nonprofits. Setting personal goals can also help bridge the gap to staying home. Choose a realistic goal such as learning a new hobby or skill.

Author's Note (Christine): I have personally made most of these changes. They were huge decisions for me, fraught with "pros and cons" lists, discussions with friends and loved ones, and hours in my head battling two people. The first says things like, "You've thought about this for years, you've planned, and there are no more questions to ask. Make the change!" And the other counters, "Well, this might not work out how you planned." This indecision is inevitable even despite thoughtful, thorough planning—rarely did I ever know for sure something was the right thing to do; I always had doubts. But being on the other side of these major changes, I can confidently say I have zero regrets and they've brought me to people, places, and experiences I couldn't have imagined. There are things I'm doing now, or people I'm close to, that never would have been possible had I not gotten my MBA years ago. Same with changing careers, changing jobs, and leaving the workplace to be with my kids. Was it easy? No. But was it worth it? Absolutely!

You'll notice some themes emerging that apply to any of these changes, including planning, networking, and self-care. When practiced regularly, these tips can make planned and unplanned transitions less stressful and more purposeful. Regular updates to your Leadership Companion through Knowing Yourself, Knowing Others, and maintaining a strong network are just a few fundamentals to ensure the success of any life choice and transition.

* * *

Additional Resources

What Color Is Your Parachute? 2017: A Practical Manual for Job-Hunters and Career-Changers, by Richard N. Bolles (Ten Speed Press, 2016).

What You're Really Meant to Do: A Road Map for Reaching Your Unique Potential, by Robert Steven Kaplan, Harvard Business Review Press, 2013.

Leadership Companion Exercise: A How To: The Five Most Common Career Changes

Assess

1. Make a list of pros and cons of a potential change you're considering, highlighting the aspects of the change that really matter. How balanced is the list?

   _____

   _____

   _____

2. Ask yourself what the worst-case scenario is for each option. Are there any you couldn't live with? How does that inform your decision?

   _____

   _____

   _____

Adapt

3. Periodically do a "health assessment" for your current job. Are you getting out of it what you'd hoped? What could you do to change the parts that you're not? Do you control the obstacles, or are they systemic?

   _____

   _____

   _____

Strategic Leadership

STRATEGIC LEADERSHIP: PREVIEW

A leader takes people where they want to go.
A great leader takes people where they don't
necessarily want to go, but ought to be.
—Rosalynn Carter

Similar to the previous section, taking on the most senior leadership roles can paradoxically call for yet a further *decrease* in your focus. Because the demands from stakeholders' priorities on you and your larger team increase exponentially, senior leaders must have few focuses: inspiring your team to a vision, establishing and reinforcing values, and ensuring the right people are on the team. You must reinforce key messages in every interaction and delegate the things you used to focus on, such as leading strategic initiatives and managing work. Your ability to accomplish this means having the right people on your team capable of receiving such advanced delegation.

Your new level of power as a more senior leader also comes with a new level of scrutiny and responsibility. Your every action and statement will be studied for intent and meaning, whether you intended for them to have meaning or not. Your organization will take its cue from what you say and do, as well as from how you do it. Harnessing this reality can be a powerful tool in shaping the direction of your organization and its culture.

Chapter 10: Senior Leadership deals with advanced leadership topics such as the role of the senior leader, including how to move beyond influencing to inspirational leadership. Because change management is a required skill for all senior leaders, this chapter also introduces adaptive change, a concept that can be useful if you need to move your organization in a new direction. Finally, this chapter covers conflict management, which can be destructive if not effectively managed.

The last two chapters in this section deal with diversity. Chapter 11 discusses what to consider when leading global teams. The growing diversity of the American workforce and the growth in multinational organizations mean that many leaders will lead or interact with teams that include members from different cultures. The final chapter in this section, chapter 12, looks at some of the challenges women and minorities face in developing into leadership positions. Decades after their entry into the workforce in large numbers, progress for women and minorities has stalled. While we leave to others the debate over whether the solution lies with organizations and their leaders or with the diverse employees themselves, we'll cover some of the common barriers to more diversity in leadership.

CHAPTER 10

Senior Leadership

*If your actions inspire others to dream
more, learn more, do more and
become more, you are a leader.*
—JOHN QUINCY ADAMS

Role of the Senior Leader

Taking on larger and more complex leadership roles, whether formally leading a large part of the organization or more informally playing a prominent leadership role as you gain experience and credibility within the organization, requires additional ability to influence and lead others outside of your official responsibilities. The people you interact with daily and lead are now more senior as well: self-starters, intelligent, great at what they do, and, perhaps most importantly, possessing their own ideas about how things should be. To grow your sphere of influence to larger and increasingly sophisticated groups in which you may not have the bandwidth, or perhaps even the opportunity, to develop and leverage personal relationships with all of them, you'll need deliberate strategies to maximize your reach. To understand the new skills you'll need, it's first important to understand how a senior leader's role is different.

Where We've Been—a Refresher

Chapter 4 explained that followers want from their leader someone who can set and execute a vision, while being trustworthy and caring.

In chapter 5, the following actions to drive team engagement were outlined:

1. Foster open communication and trust with your people.
2. Develop people predominantly through challenging team assignments or stretch projects.
3. Empower employees to act independently.
4. Set clear expectations.
5. Manage/deal with performance problems.
6. Ensure that people's strengths are in play: sometimes poor performers are just in the wrong job.

All of these basic engagement actions are still important with a larger team, but require adjustments in how you accomplish them. Most of the actions you previously took with a smaller team will now be done through the supervisors to whom your frontline team members directly report. The simple truth is that the key to managing a large team is that your supervisors, not you, are now the critical engagement link. The place to start is assessing whether they, themselves, are engaged. They may lack the skills to build engagement for their teams, but if they're engaged they'll at least want to try. If they're not engaged, however, it's unlikely their teams will be engaged. Focusing on your supervisors is now your number one people objective.

Further, now that you've built leadership skills such as coaching, emotional intelligence, and influence as explained in chapters 6, 7, and 8, and now desire to take or have taken the next step into senior leadership, you need to ensure your direct reports have, or are building, these skills.

As you focus on your management team, never forget that your time and attention are symbolically important. Where you spend your limited energy and time will be noticed by the team as indicators of what you value. You'll want to be deliberate about what you choose to engage in directly versus what you delegate to your team. Reflect on what your team needs, based on the environment or their maturity as a team, and choose to engage directly in a couple of areas in which you can make the most impact. The skills required for the senior leader build upon what you've learned so far, and the senior leader has three primary objectives:

1. To inspire your organization toward a specific and better future
2. To ensure that structure, capabilities, and processes are in place to make that future a reality
3. To set the tone, and ensure that everyone is aligned toward that future

A senior leader must still work on vision, managing performance, employee development, and communication, and we'll show you the next level for those skills. Finally, adaptive change and measurement are important tools for successful enterprise-wide transformations.

Inspirational Leadership: Nature versus Nurture

Inspirational leaders are able to motivate others to achieve more than normal, by demonstrating passion for a vision, providing others with meaning, and by understanding and aligning people's needs to a singular purpose. History is full of inspirational leaders—names like Gandhi, Martin Luther King Jr., and William Wallace. These leaders inspired their followers to accomplish much more than they thought possible.

Inspirational leaders:

- Are positive and passionate
- Create a compelling vision and get others to believe it's possible

- Help others find meaning in that vision and understand their role in fulfilling it
- Listen, are trusted by their followers, and are inclusive, so that followers feel valued and part of an effort bigger than themselves
- Have courage and will risk some degree of failure
- Dream, see a future, and are willing to try
- Recover quickly from failure, applying the learning to their next venture

It's still debated whether leaders are born with these traits or whether they can be developed. We would argue that many who "just seem to have it" weren't born with it; rather, they found what they're passionate about, which—lucky for you— is one of the exact purposes this book aims to achieve. Once you've found your passion, being inspirational tends to be more natural. Regardless of the role that genetics or experience plays in being inspirational, leaders can improve these capabilities through practice, especially since they're so aligned to the traits of effective leadership: developing as a leader will contribute to being more inspirational. Practice, first by going through the exercises of what inspires you personally and what matters to you through the Knowing Yourself exercises. Engage your team to help set a vision: listen, communicate, and help them see how they align to the organization's objectives, and see if you don't get better results and more motivated employees. You may also end up being considered an inspirational leader.

Setting the Vision

Setting the organization's vision is one of the primary roles of a senior leader. Developing vision and strategy for a larger, more complex organization is more challenging than it was when your team was smaller and your leaders set the vision and strategy for you. First, you need to deeply understand and identify the key external factors that may help or hinder your success. As the leader of a large team, you'll likely have significant latitude to set direction for your team. Outline your team's role in achieving the organization's goals, and develop a vision and strategy that help your team do its part. This is where you'll practice your forward-thinking skills, remembering that strategy is about making choices.

- Inventory your current products and services offerings. How do they compare to those of the competition? Where does your team need to be world-class in the products and services you provide, and where does it need to be low cost? What innovation will be key to leverage for growth?
- Evaluate the past: Where has your team consistently been successful, and why? Where has it consistently struggled, and why?
- What needs to change in your team to help advance the overall organization's goals?

Vision and strategy are closely related, but vision—an aspirational statement of where your organization wants to be in the future—should come first, as it provides the basis of the strategy to follow. The strategy is the long-term plan for "how" to achieve your organization's goals. Together they provide the roadmap for your organization. Involve as many people as practical in this process to increase organizational credibility of the output, include multiple perspectives, and build trust. It's generally best to focus each team on only a few key cascaded goals per year. Too many objectives can lead to scattered attention and can compromise achieving at least a few important goals. While it's common to have many tactical metrics, focusing on only a few key initiatives at a time helps everyone on the team know the most important areas to make progress on and to understand their role in making that progress happen. These activities, performed as a team, will go a long way toward aligning and building trust on your team.

Reinforcing Processes

Reinforcing processes are one of the most overlooked keys to successful execution of strategy. Reinforcing processes are those that drive and reward the desired behavior to support your vision and strategy, and they're critical to ensure support for where you want to take the organization. In order to reinforce the new direction, the organization's strategy must be incorporated into everything that touches employees. Some examples include communication strategy, employee development, employee performance evaluations and compensation, change management, organizational structure, and metrics. Other important factors include whether necessary data to measure progress against the strategy is readily available; whether training exists; and whether new processes are easy to perform and help is made available. Many strategies have derailed because alignment of their reinforcing processes was ignored. Senior leaders often aren't even aware that some of them exist. It's important for senior leaders to ensure that just as much focus and planning goes toward successful execution of the strategy as went toward creating the strategy.

Setting the Tone

One of the most crucial roles a senior leader plays is that of setting the tone for the organization. Setting the tone starts with the leader's own behavior. Organizations take significant cues from the leader, whether positive or negative. Whether the leader is generally optimistic or pessimistic, focuses on customers and employees (or not), creates fear through snap judgments and punitive actions, addresses problems, or emphasizes integrity will all be noticed by employees. Leaders also set the tone in what they choose to reward and punish. Integrity breaches, lack of accountability, or disrespectful behaviors that go unpunished will expand what's considered acceptable behavior by the organization. Tolerating poor behaviors from strong performers, who otherwise get results for the organization, will signal that results matter more than actions and can lead to bad behavior and complacency in others. This negative chain reaction often completely offsets the value from those otherwise strong performers. This ability to set the tone is a powerful leadership tool, and as the leader, you should be conscious of the tone you set in every action and communication you make.

A strong focus on others by the leader is not just healthy for the organization, but will be noticed by employees. Leaders who appear to drive their own agendas will result in organizations in which everyone looks out for themselves, while leaders who focus on others and reward those who do the same will foster an environment in which everyone pulls together toward common purposes. The courage to make tough calls and set the right tone inspires others and is a hallmark of a strategic leader.

Author's Note (Kelly): A company I worked for, which had a core value of employee safety, bought another company with a poor safety record. As our president dispersed his executive team to each of the acquisition locations to make the purchase announcement, he required us to pack and take our own plant safety equipment. I was slightly irritated at having to find room in my suitcase for a bulky hard hat, but I managed. After I made the announcement at the new plant I was assigned to, I donned my own gear and went on a plant tour, as the very first representative of the new company. As I toured, I noticed that there was a wide range of protective gear worn by the plant supervisors and employees. Though I didn't say a

*word about my observation, a stunning thing hap-
pened during the ninety minutes of my tour: somewhere along my journey through the plant, each of my
guides quietly turned up with all of the proper gear.
When I got home, I told my boss that his plan had
worked brilliantly. (He simply smiled). I'd realized what
message he was sending when he sent us with our
safety gear, but I hadn't realized just how powerful
setting the right tone would be, without my ever saying a word.*

Communication

Once your team's individual and overall objectives are outlined,
you need to communicate them. As the leader, you should play
a visible role in this communication yourself, while also allowing your supervisors to play a strong role in the communication rollout. Your supervisors will be the front lines for questions
from the employees who report to them. Involving them in the
development of those objectives ensures they can translate it
into "what it means" for their groups.

Be sure your supervisors have got it right by asking them to
practice and articulate to you what it means for their groups. As
they have the primary relationship with employees, they should
also play a key role in building support for the new direction.
It's your job to make sure that they fully understand the change,
including the "why," so that they can play a strong support role
on behalf of the change.

Communication can be one of the most impactful areas in driving engagement, so don't delegate all of it to your supervisors. Choose which messages to communicate to the team yourself. Your supervisors can most effectively deliver routine, tactical messages (the "what"), and you won't want to circumvent their critical role in being the key information provider for their employees. Strategic messages, however—the "why"—may be best communicated directly by you then reinforced over time by the supervisors.

Author's Note (Christine): I saw this concept played out successfully when serving as the HR lead for a large plant-based organization. The business unit leader was new, and immediately began every meeting—whether his direct report meetings, a one-on-one, or a town hall—with the same question, "How have you practiced safety today?" Safety was the most important goal for this organization. There were well-documented safety procedures in the plants and home office. While you expected to hear of safety issues and policy compliance in the plants, the home office employees struggled with how to support "being safe." Mostly employees spoke of not talking on their cell phones while driving (which was against company policy) or of taking extra precautions while grilling at home. One snowy winter day, I arrived to work frantic, as I'd been rear-ended during my commute. I relayed the story of being hit into traffic while trying to merge from an exit ramp. The person behind me was clearly going too fast and couldn't stop. Our plant leader said to me, "You know, all accidents are preventable." I winced, frustratedly mumbling something like, "How was I supposed to avoid getting hit from behind?" He said, "Knowing the conditions, you could have been looking in your rearview mirror to anticipate other drivers who couldn't stop." I kindly thanked him for the feedback and quickly changed the subject. But I couldn't stop thinking about what he said. He was right. I learned three big lessons here. First, our leadership was courageously living its value of safety, in every way it could, even for the office employees (me) who struggled with the safety concept. Experiencing that as an HR employee was inspiring, like I was working for some greater good, part of something bigger that thousands of employees were also striving for. Second, that advice has since saved my life—or at least a wrecked bumper—more than a handful of times. Like reacting to a hot burner when touched, I immediately look in my rearview mirror when I hit the brakes and have been able to drive out of the way of someone who was clearly going to hit me from behind. The safety team that wrote the monthly newsletter interviewed me and wrote a story about my experience. It was engaging to connect with my organization in this way; it was equally engaging for staff to see leadership living its stated values and the humility it sometimes requires to do so. Finally, while it was at times awkward and repetitive, the simple but constant attention to safety was the most important job for this business unit leader and all of us on the leadership team. That single focus translated to a cohesive, aligned leadership team, improved safety results, improved engagement, and even improved business results.

Which messages do you believe your team will want (or need) to hear directly from you? Do you have more insight or context around business updates than your supervisors? Would formal recognition be more impactful if delivered by you as the leader? If so, those may be good candidates to message yourself and not delegate. E-mail should not replace in-person or even video or phone communications. Complex or strategic messages are better communicated in person, especially at first. An irony is that, in some ways, as the environment gets more complex, leadership actually gets simpler, as the importance of in-person communication grows and directing activities decreases. Your team will want exposure to you. You are their leader, and it's important to them to see that updating them and spending time with them is important to you.

Leading Employee Development

There are few levers more impactful than development to build engagement. Developing your employees adds value to their side of the business relationship equation and demonstrates to them that their leader and organization value them. As the leader of a larger team, you'll need to accomplish this primarily through your supervisors, versus taking direct responsibility for your employees' development plans. Ensure that your supervisors understand that this is an important priority, and then build their skills in employee development. One simple way to ensure that your supervisors know the importance of employee development is by ensuring that they have strong development plans themselves. You can make development a formal goal in the context of your annual vision and strategy. By making development a documented goal, you create the necessary accountability to see that it happens, versus being a "nice to have." Help your supervisors become comfortable in developing their employees through leadership team discussions about their employee interactions and resulting development goals. You may need to spend time with your supervisors explaining basic development concepts. This book is a simple, practical place to start that education, particularly as we build to the end of the book where you'll create your own plan— you can easily share this experience with them. Depending on your team size, you may also want to consider having a development discussion with several levels down at least once or twice a year. Not only is dedicating your scarce time a highly visible way to demonstrate how important their development is to you, but you'll also have a better understanding of your supervisors' development needs. You can then coach them or match those needs to projects or exposure opportunities, both developing them and driving their engagement.

The biggest roadblock to effective employee development is that managers and employees often just can't think of what to *do* to make their development plans a reality. You have the broadest visibility of all of the work available that could develop employees, and you've developed a strong vision and strategy. Spend time brainstorming needed skills and resulting development activities related to your specific business strategy with other peers, senior leaders, and employees themselves.

Managing Performance

Just as when you were the supervisor of a small team, you must manage the performance of your larger team, even though you don't interact with all of them on a regular basis. This means tapping into your employees' strengths as well as managing poor performance. Once again, your focus for both will need to be on your frontline supervisors, and the best way to do this is to make it a point of focus with them. A regular discussion with your supervisors on their team members' strengths and opportunities from a performance perspective is one simple way to achieve that focus. Your organization's performance management cycle is one good opportunity for these discussions, though only once or twice a year is likely not often enough to provide work assignments and development opportunities to your employees based on their strengths, or to address performance issues on a timely basis.

If frontline supervisors aren't performing or don't know how to engage and develop their employees, you won't get the level of performance from your team that engaged employees deliver. Not every strong individual contributor makes a good leader of others, so hire supervisors carefully, based on what you believe about their ability to inspire and engage others. If they don't have a track record of collaboration and self-awareness, or if others don't view them as leaders, perhaps they can add more value to the organization as individual contributors. Ensure that you have a good training and development process in place, including a good role model or mentor for new supervisors, and monitor their performance closely. Poor supervisors impact not just their own performance, but also the performance of every employee who reports to them and, sometimes, others who interact with them and their teams. Your team's performance reflects on your own performance as a leader, whether positive or negative. Consider whether sacrificing your own performance is worth protecting a poor supervisor.

Adaptive Change

Senior leaders often need to get their organization to change direction and do what many don't want to do, outside of not only their comfort zones, but also perhaps outside of where the organization has proven that it can be successful. Adaptive change, a concept introduced by Ronald Heifetz in his book *Leadership without Easy Answers*, describes how leaders can affect large shifts in their constituents' perspectives.

Adaptive change is understanding and mobilizing people to address conflicts between competing goals.[48] Every organization has competing goals, and many of these produce healthy tensions within the organization, stretching it to produce more optimal results. A classic business example is the natural tension between manufacturing and sales. Manufacturing is measured on low cost, so they'll pull the organization toward producing longer runs of fewer products. Sales, on the other hand, is incented on pleasing the customer and driving sales volume. Sales will want to produce every possible product configuration that the customer can imagine. On its own, each group would tend to suboptimize the organization's profits, with too much emphasis on either cost or sales volume, but together they can work toward a more optimal balance between those conflicts, resulting in a higher profit.

Not all organizational conflict needs to be addressed by the leader (unless it's at unhealthy levels), and not all competing goals are big enough to be worth the significant effort of adaptive change. Where adaptive change may help is when an organization's environment is rapidly changing and it's becoming clear that long-term success requires the organization to adapt. Examples that could warrant the effort required for adaptive change include the rise in e-commerce, significant changes in government funding, or declines or shifts in demand. In these cases, organizations need to make significant change, adapting the existing model and culture.

In adaptive change, leaders walk the razor's edge: push too fast, and you risk determined resistance from your constituents; go too slowly, and some may revolt over a lack of progress.[49] Leaders must find the right balance of stressing the organization in the push toward change—successfully managing through that stress while those with a stake or comfort level in the status quo push back against the change. Note, successfully managing adaptive changes means bringing about the desired change; it doesn't mean that everyone will be happy or even stay. It's about bringing key influencers and the critical masses along on the journey and making progress toward the destination. Heifetz outlines five leadership principles in successfully managing adaptive change.

The first principle is deceptively obvious: defining the adaptive change. You must clearly call out the competing objectives so that the organization can recognize and understand the tensions they create. It can be easy to focus on symptoms and not on the underlying root cause of the tension. The rule of asking "why" five times as popularized in Six Sigma and other transformational process methodologies can help you get to the true root cause.[50]

The second principle in managing adaptive change is regulating the distress of the organization. Leaders do this through their own moods as well as their actions. If leaders appear concerned or stressed about the needed change, that mood will transfer to the rest of the organization. By being confident and positive about the change while acknowledging its challenges, leaders can help the organization weather the change.[51]

The third principle for leading through adaptive change is bringing disciplined attention to the key issues driving the need for change. Identify and assign actions that will push the organization a step closer to its future. Engage influential (and open-minded) employees in development of the new plan to get diverse inputs into the new direction and to create influencers who will help sell why the change is needed. As they push, senior leaders must watch for and balance the stress of change: too little may mean the change isn't aggressive enough, while too much (key people leaving or destructive behavior) may require slowing the pace of change.[52]

The final principles focus on the stakeholders of the change. The fourth principle is to give the work back to the people. Those who have to sustain the new path must eventually take responsibility for it, or the change may be permanently associated with the leader. When this happens, the initiative stops when the leader changes. Shifting the work to the employees may not be easy, as many will be rooted in the status quo. Identifying pioneers who are open to change and are influential with their peers is key. At critical moments, the leader must step in and provide visible support to these early adopters; this is the fifth and final principle. Peer pressure from those further behind on the change curve, or even the simple gravitational pull of the organization's existing processes, can discourage and eventually quiet the voices of leadership from early adopters. The leader must identify and stay close to these pioneers, learning when they are challenged and publicly protecting them in ways visible to the rest of the organization.[53]

Finally, Heifetz stresses the importance to leaders of protecting themselves during times of great stress and change. One way to do that is to focus the organization's attention on the issues and not on you. This can be a challenge, especially when you're the leading or sole voice advocating for a change. Keeping the discussion focused on the underlying issues, and not on you, helps move the organization down the change management path and helps shield you from being the center of the organization's angst. It's also important for the leader to not take personally the stress displayed by the organization. While you need to monitor and adjust the organization's distress level, it's important to remember that you are there to serve the organization's stakeholders by ensuring its long-term success. That sometimes means being unpopular. Other tips to protect yourself as the leader during adaptive change include using partners to spread the burden of change; finding a sanctuary where you can refresh; and preserving your own sense of purpose through the change.[54]

Heifetz summarizes what adaptive change needs: "Leadership...requires a learning strategy. A leader has to engage people in facing the challenge, adjusting their values, changing perspectives, and developing new habits of behavior."[55] Taking your organization through a significant change will be stressful, for the organization and for you. It won't be easy, and it will tap every leadership skill you've accumulated to date. But no one promised that being a leader is easy, and there's little more rewarding to a leader than helping your organization successfully navigate to a new and better place.

> *Author's Note (Kelly): I helped lead a change project which impacted the way over a thousand people performed one aspect of their job. The change would add a bit more work to each of those employees, making it a negative change for them. But the overall benefit to the organization was significant, saving money and solving several strategic issues and pain points that were slowing overall work down and preventing accountability. We researched the root causes of the pain points and possible solutions, developing a fact base behind our proposal. We then adopted a "sandwich" change management approach, getting senior leadership support first and then forming both a working group and key leaders from across the different affected departments to help plan and communicate the change from below and within the organization. Much care was given to choosing respected influencers for this team and helping them understand the benefits to the organization of the change. The rollout timing was calendar driven and very aggressive, especially given the sheer scale of the change, but by turning over the change to influential people deep in the affected organization and having*

them "over communicate" the change multiple times and in multiple ways, the change was on time and successful on rollout.

Getting Structure and Processes Out of the Way

Developing the best strategy in the world won't matter if you don't have what you need to implement and operate it. In fact, many senior leaders create outstanding strategies and objectives for the organization but make limited, if any, changes to the organization's structure and processes. This is a sure path to failure and frustration of the masses. As this stage requires more management skill than leadership to align the organization's elements around the strategy, some leaders choose a capable manager to lead this effort. As the leader, your job is to ensure that this work gets done and is monitored closely for effectiveness—the success of your strategy depends on it. Your organization doesn't have to be perfect to execute against your strategy, but you must have the key people, processes, systems, and data in place that are critical to your strategy. For example, if your strategy calls for mining online data to capture customer insights, you'll need equipment and data capture processes that purposefully gather the right information in usable formats, as well as people with the skills to analyze the data. If your strategy is to become the leading service provider in your industry, you'll need to spend much of your time and resources on developing good talent selection and assessment processes, excellent training for your customer-facing employees, and incentive programs aligned up and down the organization to ensure that everyone pulls in the same direction on behalf of your customers. Once you have those fantastic service people in place, the next priority is ensuring processes to appropriately compensate and listen to them to keep them engaged. Before you finalize your strategy, be sure you give thought to your organization's gaps against the strategy and develop plans to close them. Gaps that can't realistically be closed may require a scale-back in your strategy: better to succeed on a smaller scale than fail toward a larger but unrealistic goal.

Metrics

As the leader, you also need to measure progress toward and compliance with the strategy. In addition to measuring results against your strategic objective, establish diagnostic metrics that monitor the health of key processes for compliance and for any upstream issues. Communicate new targets, which will measure progress against the strategy as part of the initial communication, so that the organization will be expecting them. Establishing the right metrics is key to monitoring how an organization is learning and performing against its strategy.

A Leader's Most Valuable Tools for Success with Increased Complexity

A willingness to adapt to the needs of your organization and having people you trust around you to give you feedback increases the odds that you'll be an effective leader for your organization. Being a senior leader requires additional, complex skills—setting a vision for your organization, and then inspiring and equipping your team to accomplish that vision. You need to help navigate your team through change and manage the inevitable conflicts that arise. In spite of the additional complexity of being a senior leader, the two most useful tools to a leader at any level are *still* self-awareness and adaptability. Different situations, environments, and people will require a different leadership touch for the most effective outcome. These are the next evolutionary steps for you as a leader in knowing others and adapting appropriately. You will effectively change your habits practicing different approaches to find what works for you, in which situations and within your natural style. This energy is an investment on your part, with a real payoff. How do you do that?

- Now, more than ever, it's important to find people around you who will give you honest feedback, more challenging the higher up you go in the organization.
- Continue setting aside time to reflect on where you're not yet as effective as you'd like to be, to remind yourself why the effort is worth it.
- Go back through the insights gained from Knowing Yourself and Knowing Others, and remind yourself of

your core values and other unique leadership qualities. Be clear on the areas in which you bring unique strengths and those that might trip you up.

- Get out of the weeds: set and communicate a clear vision and expectations for your team, and follow them up with a strong focus on performance management and assignments based on your team members' strengths.
- Get in place good, skilled supervisors to maximize team performance.
- Make employee development a priority, throughout your organization.

Finding ways to build these principles into your day-to-day responsibilities and habits will quickly translate into more highly engaged employees who'll want to stay with you longer and will tell others wonderful things about working on your team. It will be more rewarding, and it may even be more fun!

* * *

Additional Resources

Leadership without Easy Answers, by Ronald A. Heifetz (Harvard University Press, 1998).

The Best Place to Work: The Art and Science of Creating an Extraordinary Workplace, by Ron Friedman, PhD (TarcherPerigee, 2015).

Managing Transitions: Making the Most of Change, by William Bridges (De Capo Lifelong Books, 2015).

Leadership Companion Exercise: Senior Leadership

Assess

1. Which elements of inspirational leadership are easiest for you? Which are the most challenging?

    _____

    _____

    _____

2. Quick vision exercise: All things considered, imagine the absolute best possible future for your team or organization. Describe in detail what that looks like, what people are saying, and what the results are.

    _____

    _____

    _____

3. What are key behavioral expectations for your team? What behaviors do you personally need to set and reinforce in order to create the right "tone"?

    _____

    _____

    _____

4. Consider reinforcing elements such as structure, pro-
    cesses, and skills. Which of these will support or impede
    advancement of your vision and strategy?

    _____

    _____

    _____

5. What are the most important messages to deliver to
    your team over the next year? Which should be deliv-
    ered directly by you, and which would be better deliv-
    ered by your supervisors? What are the most effective
    communication methods you can be using for each?

    _____

    _____

    _____

6. Identify which members of your team are top perform-
    ers with potential for larger roles or different assign-
    ments. Also identify those who are average performers
    with limited advancement potential.

    _____

    _____

    _____

Adapt

7. What one or two things can you do to be more inspira-
    tional for your team?

    a. _____

    b. _____

8. Take ideas generated in the vision exercise and come up with a one-sentence statement, which reads as if it's already happened: "We are..."

   _____

   _____

   _____

9. Conduct a goal-setting session with your team. Have everyone list his or her individual priorities. Discover themes and brainstorm aspirational goals. Answer the question, "What do we want to say about our organization a year from now?"

   _____

   _____

   _____

CHAPTER 11

Leading Global Teams

The key to community is the acceptance, in fact the celebration of our individual and cultural differences. It is also the key to world peace.

–M. Scott Peck

Why Leading Global Teams Is Important

Leadership today increasingly requires global leadership skills. Even if you don't work in a global organization, you may have customers or suppliers from or working in other countries, or your team may be made up of team members from all over the world. Depending on your role and your organization, being able to manage multicultural relationships may be advantageous, or it may be absolutely critical. The skills to lead in a global context are generally simple and can be boiled down to two basic rules: be aware of common differences in cultures, and then be open to and respectful of those differences. Skills developed in Knowing Others will come in handy here as you now apply these skills to knowing others from other countries. We'll discuss cultural differences from the perspective of leading a global team; managing other relationships, such as those with customers and suppliers, will be similar.

What's the Same?

Many of the same good leadership skills that apply to leading a local team also apply to leading global teams. All that we've discussed thus far about self-exploration, adapting, emotional intelligence, and strategic leadership come together perfectly in the context of leading global teams: those skills need to be solid habits, since the simplest things become more complex when managing across cultures. Take, for example, a first meeting with a Chinese employee, or the first dinner with a French salesperson. Simple things we take for granted like shaking hands, eye contact, table manners, or "getting to know you" topics all change once you're dealing with people from other countries. Once those basics are established—and this takes more time than with people from your own culture—learn what's important to your employees. The simple gesture of taking the time to understand what matters to them will be noticed and appreciated. If you're concerned about being too inquisitive into their personal lives, it's generally better to test the waters and demonstrate interest than not to do so. Many of your employees will be only too glad to share their culture and traditions; just be sensitive to their reactions to your initial questions and respect any reluctance on their part to share.

What's Different?

While the basic rule of showing respect and sensitivity to employee differences may be the single most valuable leadership skill in dealing with others from different cultures and countries, being aware of some basic principles in managing differences will give you a head start in knowing what to be sensitive to and ask about.

Meetings

One of the easiest ways to show respect for colleagues in other countries is scheduling teleconferences at times during everyone's workday, to the extent that it's possible. Where that isn't possible, be thoughtful and flexible in bridging the time difference. For example, a call scheduled at 06:00 EST will be 17:00 in Tokyo, allowing your Japanese employees to catch the last train home at 21:00. Avoid confusion by making note in the meeting invitation of the local time of the meeting for each party's location. Alternate the schedule of routine meetings so that participants take turns having evening calls; offer the same meeting at two or three different times in order to catch everybody at a convenient time; or rotate the times of routine meetings to trade off who is most impacted. Asian employees of American-based companies (or vice versa) are the most impacted by time differences and will particularly appreciate when you limit the impact on their personal time. Early morning and late evening teleconferences are an unavoidable fact of life for global teams; minor accommodations will help you build a cohesive global team.

Travel

Traveling with colleagues from other countries and backgrounds presents a wonderful opportunity to learn more about their experiences and practice cultural sensitivities.

- Nonwork time spent in restaurants, taxis, and airports is a great time to learn about others' backgrounds.
- Be aware that while some cultures and personalities enjoy participating in group activities or going out for a late social dinner, others do not. In selecting restaurants, be aware of any cultural food issues, such as the need for kosher food or issues with eating meat.
- Jet lag is a factor to respect in planning group activities and daily start times. When planning agendas, recognize that colleagues may not have the stamina for a long first day on their trip to another continent.

Language

Language, including body language, is another important part of being culturally sensitive. Gestures that are customary in one country can be disrespectful or even highly offensive in another. Giving and receiving items in most Asian countries should be done with two hands, palms up. Making the OK signal with the thumb and forefinger is considered rude in Brazil. Kissing the cheek of even strangers you meet is standard in most Latin American countries, while a man would never kiss a woman in public in countries with predominantly Muslim populations. In addition to gestures, eye contact practices vary across regions of the world. In America, not making eye contact can be interpreted as having something to hide, while making direct eye contact is common in Middle Eastern countries but considered rude in most of Asia. Be aware of and refrain from slang or culturally specific references in the presence of those from different backgrounds, as they may not understand them. Ensuring that everyone can participate in a conversation is respectful and creates an inclusive environment. Researching in advance the local norms and customs of the country you plan to visit can prevent you from making social errors during your visit.

Holidays

Finally, one of the smallest and perhaps most impactful acts of respect you can demonstrate to colleagues from different backgrounds is to recognize their culture's holidays and festivals. It can be frustrating to those in other countries when an American manager books a team meeting on an important cultural holiday. The minor effort involved in researching and acknowledging holidays or festivals important to your employees may well be rewarded with a measure of loyalty and engagement. You don't need to attempt to practice those holidays yourself, which could be misinterpreted or may even seem disrespectful. However, simply knowing when they are and mentioning them, as well as allowing those who report to you to take time off to be with family and to observe holidays and rituals when possible, can be meaningful and respectful gestures. The simple rules of knowing others and investing time in communication are the underlying themes for all of these actions.

Cultural Differences

While there's risk in stereotyping people or cultures, there are some distinct differences in cultural values between countries. Though there always is a wide range of individual personalities within a culture, some quite opposite the customary culture, cultural differences, which broadly apply to those from that culture, are still real. Understanding these broad differences can often help reduce the potential for conflict or tensions due to simple differences in perspective or approach. In their book *Managing Across Cultures: The Seven Keys to Doing Business with a Global Mindset*, Charlene Solomon and Michael Schell outlined seven dimensions of common cultural differences:

1. Hierarchy and egalitarianism
2. Group focus
3. Relationships
4. Communication styles

5. Time orientation
6. Change tolerance
7. Motivation—work-life balance[56]

The first of these, hierarchy and egalitarianism, has to do with how people view authority and power.[57] In countries such as Canada, Israel, and the Netherlands, people generally feel empowered to express themselves and take initiative. Opportunities for advancement are felt to be open to all. Society is more casual, and all people should be treated with the same amount of respect. The United States is closer to this empowered end of the scale. However, in countries such as India, Japan, and, to lesser degrees, Brazil and Germany, authority figures are respected and given considerable deference. You're often born into your social ranking and are expected to accept it.[58] These differences can be seen in things such as office size and styles of dress, but they also play out in less tangible ways such as people's willingness to express opinions when authority figures are present.[59] Understanding this important cultural difference and its profound implications on interactions between people from opposite ends of this spectrum can make or break those interactions.

The second dimension, group focus, relates to the importance of the individual versus the importance of the group.[60] In the United States and New Zealand, for example, the focus is on individual contribution and independence, while in South Korea and Indonesia, people identify themselves more by their affiliation with a group. In these countries, group harmony and consensus are more important to most individuals than are individual's interests.[61] This difference has implications for everything from hiring and recognition to how assignments are distributed and decisions are made. Decision-making in particular can be challenging in a multicultural group. Who's involved in making the decision, how long it takes, and how much consensus must be reached can be very different across societies, and not following expected cultural norms can be frustrating for those involved.[62]

The importance of relationships within business settings is another key difference between cultures. Canada and the United States are considered transactional cultures, where having a personal relationship with a business partner isn't always necessary. In China and Iran, however, personal relationships are paramount to conducting business. Trust must be established before business can be started, because relationships carry obligations with them. Relationships are built slowly over time; therefore, it can be difficult to break into a new market quickly in these countries.[63] There are many examples of American business failures in these strong relationship-oriented cultures, where the value of relationship was underestimated.

Communication style differences—either direct or indirect—reflect cultural values such as the importance of hierarchy and attitudes toward saving face. What you say, how much you say, and how you say it are all important components of cultural communication. Germany and Switzerland, for example, expect to-the-point communications and for decisions to be reached by the end of a meeting. In contrast, Pakistan and the Philippines value the way the message is delivered more than the message itself. Your tone, gestures, and context will be as important as your message, so you must take care to align them with the message you are delivering.[64] It's easy to see how communication differences can be a key source of misunderstanding or unintended conflict.

Time orientation indicates whether schedules or people are more important. Countries such as Spain and Thailand value relationships and people more than time; if a meeting is scheduled to end but a good discussion is underway, preserving the relationship is considered more important than holding to a schedule. Conversely, countries such as the United States and Germany, which believe that time is money, value delivering to a schedule. Deadlines don't have the same meaning to cultures that place a low value on time.[65] This is another potential source of conflict: when cultures place different values on deadlines and time management.

Change tolerance reflects how averse a culture generally is to change and innovation. Egypt and Russia, for example, are relatively averse to change, believing that much of what happens is "destiny," as opposed to the believing in the ability that they largely control their lives. Change is viewed as a threat to their values and, as such, is to be avoided. Canada and Singapore, on the other hand, believe that they are in control of their futures and expect change to occur constantly. For them, change is to be embraced and controlled.[66]

The final dimension highlighted by Solomon and Schell is motivation/work-life balance, which refers to how much achievement is valued versus a focus on personal time. Countries that value balance believe that one's personal life takes precedence over work, where high-achievement countries place emphasis on status and economic rewards. Countries such as Norway and the United Arab Emirates value a balance between these two, while countries such as China, Japan, and the United States value the status that comes with achievement above personal time. Many European countries lie somewhere in the middle, where many Latin American cultures are closer to the work/life balance end of the spectrum.[67]

As the leader of a global team seeking to learn from global experiences, you'll need to understand the cultural and personal motivations of your team members to help balance their needs with the needs of your organization. Leading or participating on a global team adds a new layer of complexity to managing the individual personalities on any team. It's important to understand some of the common pitfalls and misunderstandings that can occur. But working with and getting to know people from other countries can be deeply rewarding, helping you better understand the world around you. The challenges are worth it.

* * *

Additional Resources

Gestures: The Do's and Taboos of Body Language around the World, by Roger E. Axtell (Wiley, 2007).

The Cultural Intelligence Difference: Master the One Skill You Can't Do without in Today's Global Economy, by David Livermore PhD (AMACOM, 2011).

Leadership Companion Exercise: Leading Global Teams

Assess

1. When has someone shown you respect—or lack of respect—for some difference in your background? How did it make you feel?

   _____

   _____

   _____

Adapt

2. What differences are you familiar with in your circle of acquaintances? How can you demonstrate interest in and respect for those differences?

   _____

   _____

   _____

CHAPTER 12

Progress (and the Lack Thereof) for Women and Minorities

Diversity is not about how we differ. Diversity is about embracing one another's uniqueness.

—Ola Joseph, AUTHOR

Do We Still Care?

No overview of leadership would be complete without a discussion on diversity. Though laws prohibiting discriminatory hiring practices have been on the books for fifty years, it's disappointing that women and minorities still face challenges moving into leadership roles and receiving equal pay. We owe it to our organizations to bring focus to it whenever we can. There has been progress, and there is momentum to be leveraged, driving hope for more and improved leadership experiences for women and minorities. Because teams with more gender diversity are smarter,[68] organizations that embrace diversity may be stronger in their marketplace and may have higher growth.[69]

Next to setting vision and strategy, there may be no greater impact that a senior leader can have than ensuring diversity in the organization. To benefit from the ideas, growth, and results that a diverse team has to offer, it can help to understand the common barriers to advancement for women and minorities. Utilizing the concepts from Knowing Yourself and applying the empathy that comes with emotional intelligence, you can understand the challenges that diverse employees face and help create a culture that will remove those barriers. We'll explain the bias that exists even with the best of intentions. This awareness can fuel the honest challenge, to you and to your team, to drive and track progress in creating a diverse organization, especially among your leadership ranks.

Sheryl Sandberg's book *Lean In* did much to get both business leaders and women talking about the issues women face in advancing in the workplace. While Sandberg acknowledges that organizations and leaders have a strong role to play in advancing diversity, she focuses primarily on women's roles in adjusting their perspectives and thought processes. But the issue needs to be tackled from all angles. Here we'll focus on the role that senior leaders can play.

Why Diversity?

Demographics in the United States have shifted toward women and minorities, and with it, consumer buying power. It's perhaps stating the obvious, but a company with a diverse employee population will understand diverse customers better than will a company with a more homogenous employee base. "'Know the customer' has long been the credo of marketers and product developers, but customers are becoming more diverse... the market is definitely changing."[70]

A Deloitte report highlighted how dramatically the growth in buying power of minority communities has outpaced that of white consumers. While purchasing by whites increased by 139 percent between 1990 and 2008, spending was up 187 percent among African Americans, 349 percent for Hispanics, 337 percent for Asians, and 213 percent among Native Americans.[71] Globally, women control or influence more than 50 percent of purchases, and a same-sex partnered household makes 16 percent more shopping trips than the average US household.[72] Demographics of the labor market, along with an increasing public focus, will continue to increase pressure for companies to make progress on diversity. It's not just that women and minorities want to advance to more senior positions, but the marketplace is beginning to demand it. For example, Morgan Stanley clients say they want to see more diversity among Morgan Stanley bankers and salespeople.[73] This is quickly becoming more than theoretical: the marketplace increasingly demands it of suppliers, with 90 percent of Standard & Poor's companies having supplier diversity policies requiring a certain percentage of suppliers to be owned by women or minorities.[74] Women are already turning to self-employment and start-ups to master their schedule with children more effectively; *The Atlantic* magazine cited a report from the Women's Policy Research (IWPR) that showed that women are steadily increasing their presence in the world of small-business ownership. "About 29 percent of America's business owners are women, that's up from 26 percent in 1997. The number of women-owned firms has grown 68 percent since 2007, compared with 47 percent for all businesses."[75] Additionally, minority women–owned businesses have grown 265 percent since 1997.[76] Minority-owned businesses are also growing rapidly. According to the US Bureau of the Census, there were 8 million minority-owned firms in 2012, up from 5.8 million, or 38.1 percent, from 2007.[77]

Barriers to Diversity

Progress Has Stalled

A key barrier for women and minorities who want to advance is the difficulty in getting there. Many organizations track the progress of women and minorities, identify those with "high potential," require that the applicant pool include them, and set targets for their placement in leadership. Yet, for all of the increased activity, according to Catalyst, these efforts aren't yielding a material number of more women executives; in fact, progress has recently stalled. According to Catalyst, women held only 19.9 percent of S&P 500 corporate board seats in 2016, flat with 2015.[78] And only 4.4 percent of CEO positions were held by women, also with no year-over-year growth.[79] According to The Center for American Progress, women of color face even a larger gap. In 2013, women of color made up 36 percent of the female labor force and 17 percent of the total labor force and are currently 16.5 percent of workers in S&P 500 companies. However, they account for only 3.9 percent of executive-or senior-level officials and managers in those companies.[80]

"I'm Not Qualified"

Human nature itself is also a barrier to the advancement of women. There are many studies that show differences in confidence between men and women when applying for jobs. For example, men may apply for a job or "put their name in the hat" when they feel they meet as little as 20 percent of the job's qualifications. Conversely, women will only apply when they feel they meet at least 80 percent of its qualifications. Jenna Goudreau from *Forbes* cleverly stated, "Women round down and men round up."[81] And so we're missing out on a lot of women for most jobs. Being 20 percent qualified is perhaps *exactly* when women should apply. It means you'll be stretched and will grow and advance your skills more quickly, which is exactly what aspiring executives need. It also shows superiors and hiring managers that you want to grow and will take risks.

YOU ARE BORN TO LEAD

Unconscious Bias

Most people find it uncomfortable to acknowledge that we're all fundamentally hard-wired for bias. Unaddressed, biases can have detrimental effects in the workplace. What is unconscious bias? According to a white paper published by UNC Kenan-Flegler Business School, "The Real Effects of Unconscious Bias in the Workplace," unconscious bias is how our brain evolved to mentally group things together to help make sense of the world.

> The brain categorizes all the information it is bombarded with and tags that information with general descriptions it can quickly sort information into. Bias occurs when those categories are tagged with labels like "good" or "bad" and are then applied to entire groups. Unconscious bias can also be caused by conditional learning. For example, if a person has a bad experience with someone they categorize as belonging to a particular group, they often associate that entire group with that bad experience.[82]

Unconscious biases in the workplace can skew talent and performance reviews and can affect who gets hired, promoted, and developed. It may also explain the stalled progress of women and minorities in leadership positions. "A 2015 Pew Research Center survey found that 40 percent of respondents said there were double standards for women who wanted entry into the C-suite."[83] A few of the unconscious biases that directly impact the workplace include:

- Affinity bias: the tendency to like people who are like ourselves
- Halo effect: the tendency to think that everything about a person is good because you like that person
- Perception bias: the tendency to form stereotypes and make subjective assumptions about certain groups
- Confirmation bias: the tendency for people to look for information which confirms preexisting beliefs or assumptions
- Group think: this bias occurs when people try too hard to fit into a particular group by mimicking others or holding back thoughts and opinions, robbing their organizations of their full creativity and innovation[84]

The first place to start in addressing unconscious biases is to acknowledge that they exist. Senior leaders can play a strong role in challenging them by challenging human resources processes as well as the assumptions that they and their supervisors are making when they recruit and select new team members.

How to Measure Progress

Your human resources department may be already providing you with diversity data. Capturing and monitoring such data is critical to understanding your organization's gaps objectively so that you can set meaningful goals. If you don't have this data, ask to get it. Tracking total numbers and percentages of men, women, and minorities against the following should be enough to get meaningful information:

- Total organization
- Grade, level, or position, particularly individual contributor and first-line, midlevel, and executive-level managers
- Talent assessment ratings (e.g., nine-box ratings or other data used to manage talent and potential)
- Performance ratings
- Pay decisions, particularly the outliers, for each group against performance ratings
- Turnover rates

Creating a Diverse Culture

Basic awareness of the barriers for diverse employees is the first step to removing them. Raising awareness of unconscious bias among your hiring managers can bring objectivity into the hiring and promotion process, and tracking of key metrics will drive accountability. Most importantly, building diversity into and driving bias out of your core people processes are the best ways to deliver and sustain progress with diversity. Some ideas for driving momentum toward creating a diverse culture include:

1. Holding focus groups with your diverse employees to understand their concerns, and experiences, and, most importantly, to explore potential solutions.

2. Consider requiring your leaders to have regular, meaningful conversations with diverse employees about their career aspirations, development, and growth.

3. Requiring your leaders to actively develop diverse employees as part of your succession planning process.

4. Addressing bias in hiring and promotion decisions by providing objective interview guides, requiring diverse candidate pools, and building diverse interview panels.

5. Using an objective facilitator to debrief candidate interviews to ensure fact-based decisions are made.

Finally, as you succeed in hiring and promoting diverse employees, don't congratulate yourself too soon. Diverse employees are often hired but then don't stay, because the culture doesn't value different opinions, styles, or approaches. Be a champion for fostering an open culture and welcoming multiple perspectives where diverse employees can thrive.

As with strategy, vision, and values, a leader who understands the workplace barriers for diverse employees, addresses unconscious bias openly, builds removal of those barriers into the organization's core processes, and holds other leaders accountable for progress using facts will create a culture where a wide variety of people want to work, and which has a better chance of success in an increasingly diverse marketplace.

* * *

Additional Resources

Good Is Not Enough: And Other Unwritten Rules for Minority Professionals, by Keith R. Wyche (Portfolio, 2009).

Nice Girls Don't Get the Corner Office: 101 Unconscious Mistakes Women Make That Sabotage Their Careers, by Lois P. Frankel (Hachette Book Group, 2014).

Lean In: Women, Work, and the Will to Lead, by Sheryl Sandberg (Alfred A. Knopf, 2013).

Talking from 9 to 5: Women and Men at Work, by Deborah Tannen (William Morrow Paperbacks, 2001).

Leadership Companion Exercise: Progress (and the Lack Thereof) for Women and Minorities

Assess

1. In what ways might you personally have unconscious bias? What about your organization?

   _____

   _____

   _____

2. Consider your customers, vision, and strategy. In what ways do you need to be more diverse?

   _____

   _____

   _____

3. What successes have you had with diversity efforts or diverse employees? What benefits did it bring to your team and organization?

   _____

   _____

   _____

4. Imagine the perfect, diverse team: in thought, perspective, gender, minorities, etc. What does it look like? What benefits would it bring to your team and organization?

   _____

   _____

   _____

Adapt

5. Name one action you can take to address your own un-conscious biases.

   _____

   _____

   _____

6. Share your "ideal diverse team" with your boss, HR leader, or a trusted peer. Get input on potential actions you can take to move toward this ideal.

   _____

   _____

   _____

CHAPTER 13

Bringing It All Together

What are you going to do to make
the world awesome? Well nothing
if you keep sittin' there!

–KID FOR PRESIDENT

By now you're well armed with knowledge about yourself, your current circumstances, and how you can start adapting and leading right where you are now and into the future. Now all you need is a plan to bring it all together.

In our experience, "development plans" too often get only a halfhearted effort, after which they spend most of their obsolete life in a drawer. We want you to see the value you can get from completing and regularly reflecting on the exercises in this book, which were thoughtfully chosen after years of experience developing (and not developing) ourselves and others. You've been completing the Leadership Companion: a living, breathing narrative about your unique story. This can be your plan, your holistic roadmap to daily guide you toward your short- and long-term goals and dreams. You've already started working at it, having completed all of the exercises in this book, and now you'll bring it to life. We've included a template at the end of the chapter, along with steps to walk you easily and deliberately through the process of creating your customized plan.

> *Author's Note (Christine): The one or two times I actually had someone ask me to create a development plan or ask me what I wanted to do next, I tried to ignore them. If it was required, I put very little time into it, always using the crutch, "Well, my job is challenging enough." Frankly, at times, particularly when I had small children, this might actually have been true. I couldn't fathom putting any more effort toward my career. But I was wrong. I was having a pretty good career based on hard work and luck—the same recipe we recommend against. But I looked around and saw others really flourishing, and what I realized is that they knew who they were, where they were headed, and what they wanted to do. I always envied that "quality," only to discover that the people I respected as leaders had deliberately engaged in development activities, asked for feedback, allowed themselves to be mentored, set goals, and stayed true to themselves.*

One trap into which people commonly fall is getting stuck navigating through two common realities: short-term goals, which are generally related to your current job, and long-term, "If money weren't an issue, I would…" dreams. It's important and possible to honor both, and to whatever extent possible, you should focus on development activities that apply to both. Avoid holding yourself back with limiting beliefs and assumptions as you develop your plan, for example, "I can't move to consulting because I make too much money in my current job," or "I can't take a job with more responsibility because I have small children," or "I can't get into sales job because I didn't grow up in sales." At this stage, just write down that dream and keep an eye on it. Remember, this is about becoming someone—your unique leadership self—and those nudges from your soul deserve some ink, too.

Your plan will include these characteristics:

1. Long-term "dream" goals, five to ten years out
2. Short-term goals that help build your unique self where you are today and prepare you for what you want to do next
3. Goals that build on your existing strengths
4. Specific goals that allow you to "see" the result
5. Built-in accountability
6. Goals that energize and excite you

Defining your goals is often the hardest part of a development plan, as many people struggle with knowing what they want to do. However, the work you've done so far has prepared you to start being your unique leadership self right now *and* will make the part where you set your goals much easier.

Write it Down and Watch It Happen—Dream Goals

The simple act of writing down goals rarely gets the credit it deserves for setting the right things in motion. When you write down goals, dreams, or ideas, you develop images, feelings, and excitement in your brain that—magnet-like—lead you to act in line with those goals. Without goals, it can be easy to get distracted.

For now, think of one or two aspirational goals taken either directly or thematically from the Leadership Companion exercises. For example, look back at the "ideal life" exercise in chapter 2. That may very well be your long-term, dream goal. Or, maybe other ideas emerged throughout the book and exercises that inform a big idea for where you'd like to be in the future. Do not judge or overthink these idea gems!

Short-Term Goals

Reviewing the exercises in the book is the first step to constructing the actions that will bring you to becoming your unique leadership self. Here are some other similar questions to consider:

- What are examples of things you'd like to do in the future? For example, manage large projects, lead people, work on an acquisition, or gain international experience. For each of these, answer, "Why?" It's the perfect opportunity to pause and make sure that these ideas are consistent with your values and other learnings from the Leadership Companion exercises, and aren't superficial desires. Being clear about your intent also discourages you from blindly applying for every job that's a promotion. Not being clear about this can not only land you in a role which may not be a good fit, but may also earn you a reputation as someone more concerned about advancing than about being in a role in which you can benefit your organization.

- What feedback have you received from others, formal or informal, about areas that you should improve upon that might get in the way of this goal?

- What are projects and situations where you've performed well versus those where you struggled? Brainstorm a list of everything you can think of, including both strengths and opportunities, which may be the seed of a goal you want to work on.

From this information, narrow your brainstormed list to, at most, three development focus areas for the next six to eighteen months. Focusing on a few impactful areas will move you closer to your goals than making no progress against a long list.

The best development activities are tied to an existing business strategy as well as personal interests. Some common on-the-job development experiences include:

- "Scope" assignments with increased process, function, product, global, or people responsibilities
- Being assigned to a turnaround project
- Participating in more executive-level planning, analysis, or committee involvement
- Leading a project team tied to business strategy; presenting at key executive meetings
- Being a backup for someone more senior
- Joining a board of directors
- Leading a team with global team members and visiting those locations

Which of the ideas on your list would be the most impactful if you improved them? Are there any strong themes across the list, positive or negative, which are either key strengths to build on or key barriers to address? Also look for relationships between the items on your list that may make sense to combine. It's common for our weaknesses to be flip sides of our strengths, when we overuse them. You may want to work on these together, continuing to build your strength while learning to mitigate its downside. Note long-term goals, dreams, and ideas on the list, working to ensure that your short-term objectives will in some way bring you closer to those as well.

Author's Note (Kelly): I once transferred to a team where no one had development plans; I informed them that I would help them all develop them. One of the supervisors had thirty-nine years with the company. When I sat down with her to discuss hers, she immediately asked me if she had to have one, as she'd already let us know that she intended to retire in eighteen months. I told her that yes, she did, though I have to admit I had silent doubts about insisting. But I asked her one simple question: after thirty-nine years with the company, what did she want to accomplish in her last eighteen months? She had an immediate and amazing answer: she told me that when she retired, she wanted those "young'uns" (that's a quote) to be able to take over her duties seamlessly. You see, she was one of those rare people who really ran the business, and she knew what she knew. Best of all, after thirty-nine years she cared enough about the business and the team that she wanted her retirement to not cause a ripple. So this awesome lady developed her first, and last, development plan at the thirty-nine-year mark in her career. It contained only one goal—knowledge transfer—but when she retired eighteen months later, it was smooth. She executed her development plan with passion because it was her goal, and it mattered to her. I've told her story dozens of times: if development makes sense for someone at the thirty-nine-year mark in her career, do any of us have an excuse not to work toward our own goals?

Build on Your Strengths

Your strengths are what make you special and have made you successful so far; it only makes sense to keep building on them. Weaknesses should only be included in your development plan if they're barriers that are preventing you from achieving your goals. Weaknesses generally can't be turned into strengths; they can only be improved enough to limit their impact. Therefore, you should focus only on weaknesses that are standing in the way of what you want to get done. Your strengths will continue to drive your success; never stop building on them. They set you apart from others and help you become your best self.

To Train or Not to Train

A common misperception is that developing yourself means a list of training classes. While training has a place in development plans, it's the least effective type of learning for adults and should play the smallest role. Many organizations recommend the 70/20/10 rule for development, reported by Lombardo and Eichinger in their book *The Career Architect Development Planner*: "Development generally begins with a realization of current or future need and the motivation to do something about it." This may come from several sources, including feedback, making a mistake, or watching others' behaviors and actions. They continue, "The odds are that development will be about 70 percent from on-the-job experiences and working on tasks and problems, about 20 percent from feedback or working around good and bad examples of the need, and 10 percent from courses and reading."[85]

Vague Stays in the Drawer—Get Specific

Getting your goals written down in language that's clear and measurable takes some practice. Though challenging, this step is important because of the thought process and conservations that result, particularly with your supervisor.

Internationally recognized 1960s research by Dr. Edward Locke, later expanded on for the workplace by Dr. Gary Latham, showed that clear goals and appropriate feedback motivate employees. Locke went on to highlight that working toward a goal is also a major source of motivation, which, in turn, improves performance. Locke's research showed that the more difficult and specific the goal, the harder people tend to work to achieve it.[86] Action is action, and this is an ongoing process. Don't use your current difficulty in articulating your goals as a reason to not do anything. Doing something—anything—tends to lead to other ideas and actions.

Your goals should be broad enough to be impactful, but not so broad that they aren't well defined. "Being an influential leader" or "learning spreadsheets" are too broad, while "taking a presentation class" is too narrow. Think about the "why" if your initial goal is too narrow, which may point to a broader theme. The presentation class example could instead become "Improve presentation skills to influence others with my ideas" or "Become proficient at presenting, as evidenced by closed sales deals." If it's truly a one-off item that isn't part of a broader, impactful focus, strike it from your plan (excluding it doesn't mean that you can't take the class). For goals that are too broad, make them more specific, being as clear as possible about what you want to accomplish. This can be challenging, particularly for soft skills such as leadership, communication, or influencing. Framing goals in a SMART format that can be measured is the next step. SMART goals, introduced by George T. Doran in 1981, help you write objectives so they are achievable:[87]

<u>S</u>pecific
<u>M</u>easurable
<u>A</u>ttainable
<u>R</u>elevant
<u>T</u>imely

Here are two examples of weak and strong development goals, and corresponding measurements:

Weak	Strong	Measurement
Become a more influential leader.	Further develop influential leadership skills, so that my voice is heard on projects, and my peers seek me out for coaching; or, further develop my influential leadership skills so that I can lead my team through change more quickly and effectively.	The measurements for these goals will be examples of influencing project results, being sought out for coaching, or surpassing project goals for a change transition.
Collaborate with key stakeholders.	Improve collaboration with key groups by building relationships with targeted Sales, Product Development, and Operations stakeholders, becoming the go-to resource for them from our department; or, improve collaboration with R&D and Marketing so that we can close X percent more new business this year.	The measurements for these goals will be success in becoming a go-to resource or achieving the new business goal.

For each of these examples, the strong goals make it clear what this leader is trying to accomplish and how they will measure success. At the end of the year, examples of progress should be easy to identify, and it should be clear whether progress was made.

Don't Go It Alone—Build in Accountability

Your supervisor has an important role to play. They can give you feedback on your focus areas early in the process, to ensure that you're focusing on areas your organization values and which are aligned with its business strategy. As you get them into a SMART format, have a discussion with your supervisor to help identify projects and opportunities for you to develop those skills and identify any resources you'll need from others.

Whatever the normal planning cycle is for your organization is great timing to consider development opportunities: executing organization goals for the year in conjunction with employee development planning provide a very strategic, "just in time" workforce planning approach, ensuring a focus on development during the very time projects are being planned and resources assigned for the year. Senior leaders can help identify those 70 percent hands-on opportunities, and they're also in the best position to commit resources. They're a critical resource to be tapped during any people development planning effort.

In addition to your immediate supervisor, consider engaging an accountability partner to help you through this. It could be a peer, a mentor, or a friend or colleague...anyone you can check in with regularly and with whom you're willing to share this exercise. Research conducted by Leigh Stringer, author of *The Healthy Workplace*, showed that healthy, outcome-based organizations were using peer-based partnerships for personal and business goals.[88] Stringer writes,

> Compared to mentorship—a more hierarchical relationship—a peer-to-peer relationship seems to be easier to organize, and it's a more effective tool for making progress towards a goal. Accountability partnerships work when they're a collaboration between two colleagues who like and respect one another—your partner is someone you trust, who will keep you honest and moving on a path you set for yourself.

What do you do if you can't find a way to achieve your goals within your current role or elsewhere in the organization? Or, worse, if your organization doesn't show support for development activities? In this case, talk to others outside your organization who can provide input and ideas. These might be industry peers, friends of friends, or family whom you think have skills, knowledge, or connections in the area of development you seek. This does the double duty of expanding your network and furthering your path to achieving your goals.

Nonprofit boards or other nonprofit roles are also great opportunities to gain broadening experiences, although often on your own time.

Excitement Equals Action

Your Leadership Companion will help focus you on what you need to work on to achieve your goals. You should be passionate about the goals in them, because the more passion you have for them, the more energy you'll be willing to put toward accomplishing them.

Were your goals as specific as possible? Could you see them? Were you excited about them? Many development goals aren't completed in a year, or even in a career. Sometimes they fizzle out, and that's OK. Maybe the actions weren't specific enough. Maybe you weren't as tied to that goal as you'd thought. Regardless, all thoughtful actions move you closer toward knowing yourself better, toward growth and more purposeful work.

It's common to carry over goals to two or more years, though the focus will often shift, as you make progress in some areas. A complete refresh of your goals, replacing old ones and adding new ones, should be done at least once a year.

Author's Note (Christine): I've had a list of goals going back years. Many I've joyfully crossed off, and a few I begrudgingly rewrote to try again the next year, paying close attention to "Why didn't I complete this? Did I not give it priority? Were the actions too vague? Am I not really passionate about it anymore?" On these, I go back and review my Leadership Companion exercise responses, even do a few of them again, to gain additional insights and inspiration. Then, I start the year again, knowing I'm moving closer and closer to my long-term goals and feeling excited about the short-term goals I'll have achieved in the coming year.

* * *

Additional Resources

Strengths Based Leadership: Great Leaders, Teams, and Why People Follow, by Tom Rath and Barry Conchie (Gallup Press, 2008).

Developing the Leader within You, by John C. Maxwell (Thomas Nelson, 2005).

Being the Boss: The 3 Imperatives of Becoming a Great Leader, by Linda A. Hill and Kent Lineback (Harvard Business Review Press, 2011).

Leadership Companion Exercise: Developing Yourself

Assess

1. Brainstorm a list of potential development goals, including both short-term (twelve to twenty-four months) and long-term/aspirational. Consider the Leadership Companion exercises, the feedback you've received on both strengths and opportunities, and organization/team goals.

    _____

    _____

    _____

Adapt

2. Review your brainstormed list, choosing a maximum of three. Consider relationships between them, and decide which are likely to be the most impactful toward helping you achieve your goals. Using the template provided, create your Leadership Companion Action Plan.

    _____

    _____

    _____

3. Review and refine your chosen goals with your supervisor and trusted accountability partner.

_____

_____

_____

Scaling for Organizations

Consider adding to existing compensation, performance, talent review, or annual business planning processes a discussion of how to match up specific employee development needs to business or strategic projects. Or, create development opportunities for your group, such as completing this book together.

Leadership Companion Action Plan

Review the examples below. Then, create your own plan with the provided template. You can even include personal goals in this simple, effective format.

Goals (specific/ measurable)	Which aspect(s) of knowing self and knowing others does this goal support? (e.g., core values, inspiration, peak moments, culture, serving others, networking, etc.)	Action Plan
By September, I will run a 10k in under fifty-four minutes.	Getting regular exercise	1. Sign up for a race 2. Download 10k training plan 3. Tell my friend Margo and report progress

By X time, I will position myself for a future promotion.	Doing work I love that fits with my values	1. Identify people with whom I worked well, and with whom I enjoyed working, in the past 2. Discuss with my boss internal people with whom to informally network 3. Identify specific work or projects that will increase my skills for the next level
By X time, I will pitch my idea about X improvement to the leadership team.	Feeling valued; continuous improvement	1. Identify and rank key stakeholders and their expected concerns and benefits 2. Present to supervisor and brainstorm next steps
By X time, I will...		

Leadership Companion Action Plan

Create your own action plan with the following blank template. You may also download a blank template and the Leadership Companion exercises at www.mclarenconsulting.net/book.

Goals (specific/ measurable)	Which aspect(s) of knowing self and knowing others does this goal support? (e.g., core values, inspiration, peak moments, culture, serving others, networking, etc.)	Action Plan

CONCLUSION

Inspired and Ready to Lead

Congratulations! In reading this book and spending time on the Leadership Companion exercises and action plan, you've accomplished something most of your colleagues have not: you've built the foundation of becoming your most unique leadership self and creating your brand and voice.

Now develop a habit of going back and reviewing your Leadership Companion that's consistent with your personality...at least quarterly, if that's your style, or informally when needed. It's been surprising to look back at previous iterations of plans, and see that what we were focusing on in the past has become second nature now. Here are some ideas:

How?

- First, get a folder or three-ring binder where you can keep the book, notes, printouts of inspiring articles, Leadership Companion exercises, copies of your goal template, https://mclarenconsulting.net/book/, and any other notes. The point is to have anything and everything possible around your leadership journey in one compact, easily transportable location.

- You can also keep track of your plan and documents in a folder on your digital notebook, phone, or computer.
- Consider continuing on this journey with an accountability partner. This could be a co-worker, spouse, or friend. Establish a plan for the two of you, or a group, to work through your plans as a team.

When?

- At least annually, review your Leadership Companion and goals to determine if you've had any goal changes, to identify new challenges you'd like to work on for the upcoming year, and to celebrate the achievement of your goals!
- When a job change represents a significant change in responsibilities.
- When you're under a significant amount of stress.
- When things just don't seem to be going well in your job.
- During a significant career transition.
- When you receive significant feedback as part of a 360 feedback process or a mentoring discussion, from a boss or co-worker, or during a performance review.

We hope by now that you've started to see that the true path to leadership is to discover and apply your most unique leadership self. We intended for this book to act as an accelerator, introducing you to many leadership lessons just in time, or even in advance of when you'll be tackling them. By equipping you with the most common leadership lessons and some basic tools to help you think through and practice them in real time, we hope to help you advance through them faster, and with fewer mistakes, than we have. We've invested this effort in you because you, and the people you lead, are worth it.

We believe you'll have the most success in your career and in all aspects of life when you're working toward goals, applying your strengths, and operating within your values. We hope that, knowing more about and fully appreciating your unique leadership qualities, voice, and brand, you will apply them to making an impact both right now and toward more exciting things in the future. It's a journey, no doubt, but one we hope to have inspired you to jump on and stay on—you're so worth it!

* * *

BIBLIOGRAPHY

"9 Things Employees Want from Their Managers (and 5 Things They Don't)." *HR Specialist.* Accessed February 6, 2017. http://www. thehrspecialist.com/article.aspx?articleid=32033&cigx=d. nac, stid.2942, sid.115314, lid.11, mid.1708.

Akitunde, Anthonia. "Back to School: What You Must Think about before Furthering Your Education after 50." *Huffington Post.* August 17, 2012. http://www.huffingtonpost.com/2012/08/17/ back-to-school-adult-education-student-loans_n_1773801. html.

Bacon, Terry R. *What People Want: A Manager's Guide to Building Relationships.* Mountain View, CA: Davies-Black Publishing, 2006.

Burg, Natalie. "Businesses Harness the Power of Diversity for Growth." *Forbes.* December 24, 2013. https://www.forbes. com/sites/capitalonespark/2013/12/24/businesses-harness-the-power-of-diversity-for-growth/#6400b1a0b91f.

"Career Change Statistics: You Will Change Careers 7 Times in Your Life?" Careers Advice Online. Accessed February 5, 2017. http://www.careers-advice-online.com/career-change-statistics.html.

Chen, Catherine. "Effective Leadership: How to Not Take Things Personally." *Huffington Post*. November 7, 2013. http://www.huffingtonpost.com/catherine-chen-phd/effective-leadership-how-_b_4226286.html.

"Corporate Culture." *Inc. Magazine*. Accessed February 8, 2017. www.inc.com/encyclopedia/corporate-culture.html.

Costigan, Amelia. "5 Facts You Need to Know about Buying Power." *Catalyst*. May 20, 2015. http://www.catalyst.org/zing/-5-facts-you-need-know-about-buying-power.

Doran, George T. "There's a S.M.A.R.T. Way to Write Management's Goals and Objectives." *Management Review*, Vol. 70, Issue 11, 1981.

Duggan, Kris. "Why the Annual Performance Review is Going Extinct." *Fast Company*. October 20, 2015. https://www.fastcompany.com/3052135/the-future-of-work/why-the-annual-performance-review-is-going-extinct.

Goleman, Daniel. "What Makes a Leader?" *Harvard Business Review*, January 2004.

———. *Working with Emotional Intelligence*. New York: Bantam Books, 1998.

Gottman, John M., PhD. *The Seven Principles for Making Marriage Work: A Practical Guide from the Country's Foremost Relationship Expert*. New York: Three Rivers Press, 1999.

Goudreau, Jenna. "Why Do Women Round Down While Men Round Up?" *Forbes*. January 11, 2012. http://www.forbes. com/sites/jennagoudreau/2012/01/11/women-round-down-confidence-career-advancement/#407bf50423e9.

Hall, John. "10 Ways to Help Others That Will Lead You to Success." *Fortune*. May 26, 2013. http://www.forbes.com/ sites/johnhall/2013/05/26/10-ways-to-help-others-that-will-lead-you-to-success/#481b3e471e4f.

Heifetz, Ronald A. *Leadership without Easy Answers*. Cambridge, MA: The Belknap Press of Harvard University Press, 1997.

Hersey, Paul and Blanchard, Kenneth H. and Johnson, Dewey E. *Management of Organizational Behavior: Leading Human Resources*. Upper Saddle River, NJ: Prentice Hall, Inc., 2001.

Hill, Linda A. and Kent Lineback. *Being the Boss: The 3 Imperatives of Becoming a Great Leader*. Boston: Harvard Business Review Press, 2011.

Horrigan, John B. "Lifelong Learning and Technology." Pew Research Center. March 22, 2016. http://www.pewinternet.org/2016/03/22/lifelong-learning-and-technology/.

Kruse, Kevin. "What is Employee Engagement?" *Forbes.* June 22, 2012. http://www.forbes.com/sites/kevinkruse/2012/06/22/employee-engagement-what-and-why/#243c43a84629.

LaCapra, Lauren Tara. "Morgan Stanley CFO Says Companies Need More Female Executives." *Reuters.* April 2, 2014. http://www.reuters.com/article/2014/04/03/morganstanley-porat-idUSL1N0MV03N20140403.

Laluyaux, Fred. "Perception vs. Reality: Do You Know What Your Real Company Culture Is?" *Inc. Magazine.* October 13, 2014. http://www.inc.com/fred-laluyaux/perception-vs-reality-do-you-know-what-your-real-company-culture-is.html.

Locke, Edwin A. "Motivation Through Conscious Goal Setting." *Applied & Preventative Psychology* 5(1996). https://www.researchgate.net/profile/Edwin_Locke/publication/222720003_Motivation_through_Conscious_Goal_Setting/links/00b4952d42aa12d430000000.pdf.

"Los Angeles County a Microcosm of Nation's Diverse Collection of Business Owners, Census Bureau Reports." US Bureau of the Census. December 15, 2015. http://www.census.gov/newsroom/press-releases/2015/cb15-209.html.

Michael M. Lombardo and Robert W. Eichinger. *Career Architect Development Planner*, 4th ed. Minneapolis, MN: Lominger International, 2007.

McCormick, Horace. "The Real Effects of Unconscious Bias in the Workplace." UNC Kenan-Flagler Business School (2015): 5. http://www.kenan-flagler.unc.edu/~/media/Files/documents/executive-development/unc-white-paper-the-real-effects-of-unconscious-bias-in-the-workplace-Final.

McLaren, Christine. "Knowing Yourself First, Part I." *Monday Mentor*. June 25, 2012. https://mondaymentor.wordpress.com/2012/06/25/knowing-yourself-first-part-i/.

———. "Knowing Yourself First, Part II." *Monday Mentor*. June 30, 2012. https://mondaymentor.wordpress.com/2012/06/30/knowing-yourself-first-part-ii/.

Paul, Alison Kenney, Thom McElroy, and Tonie Leatherberry. "Diversity as an Engine of Innovation." Deloitte University Press. January 1, 2011. http://dupress.com/wp-content/uploads/2011/01/US_deloittereview_Diversity_as_an_Engine_of_Innovation_Jan11.pdf.

Peters, Tom. "The Brand Called You." *Fast Company.* August 31, 1997. https://www.fastcompany.com/28905/brand-called-you.

Rath, Tom and Barry Conchie. *Strengths Based Leadership: Great Leaders, Teams, and Why People Follow.* New York: Gallup Press, 2008.

Rath, Tom. *StrengthsFinders 2.0.* Washington, DC: The Gallup Organization, 2007.

Robinson, Rob. "Four Diversity Supplier Reporting Trends." *Wharton Magazine.* May 14, 2005. http://whartonmagazine.com/blogs/four-supplier-diversity-reporting-trends/.

Shoemaker, Jolynn, Amy Brown, and Rachel Barbour. "A Revolutionary Change: Making the Workplace More Flexible." *Solutions Journal* 2(2011): 52–62. http://www.thesolutionsjournal.com/node/889.

Smallwood, Norm. "Define Your Personal Leadership Brand in Five Steps." *Harvard Business Review.* March 29, 2010. https://hbr.org/2010/03/define-your-personal-leadership.

Snyder, Benjamin. "Half of Us Have Quit Our Job Because of a Bad Boss." *Fortune.* April 2, 2015. http://fortune.com/2015/04/02/quit-reasons/http://fortune.com/2015/04/02/quit-reasons/.

Solomon, Charlene M. and Michael S. Schell. *Managing Across Cultures: The Seven Keys to Doing Business with a Global Mindset*. New York: McGraw Hill, 2009.

Sorenson, Susan and Keri Garman. "How to Tackle U.S. Employees' Stagnating Employee Engagement." *Gallup Business Journal*. June 11, 2013. http://www.gallup.com/businessjournal/162953/tackle-employees-stagnating-engagement.aspx.

Stanier, Michael Bungay. *Do More Great Work: Stop the Busywork. Start the Work That Matters*. New York: Workman Publishing Company, Inc., 2010.

Stillman, Jessica. "Why Accountability Partners Beat Mentors." *Inc. Magazine*. April 5, 2016. http://www.inc.com/jessica-stillman/what-beats-a-mentor-an-accountability-partner.html.

Stringer, Leigh. "The Essential Ingredient You're Missing in Achieving Your Goals." *Huffington Post*. June 9, 2016. http://www.huffingtonpost.com/entry/the-essential-ingredient-youre-missing-in-achieving-your-goals_us_5730ecc3e4b016f37896af06.

Thompson, Jeff, PhD. "Is Nonverbal Communications a Numbers Game?" *Psychology Today*. September 30, 2011. https://www.

psychologytoday.com/blog/beyond-words/201109/is-non-verbal-communication-numbers-game.

Warner, Judith. "The Women's Leadership Gap: Women's Leadership by the Numbers." Center for American Progress. August 4, 2015. https://www.americanprogress.org/issues/women/report/2015/08/04/118743/the-womens-leadership-gap/.

White, Gillian. "Women Are Owning More and More Small Businesses." *The Atlantic.* April 17, 2015. http://www.theatlantic.com/business/archive/2015/04/women-are-owning-more-and-more-small-businesses/390642/.

"Women on Corporate Boards Globally." *Catalyst.* January 4, 2017. http://www.catalyst.org/knowledge/women-corporate-boards-globally.

"Women CEOs of the S&P 500." *Catalyst.* January 3, 2017. http://www.catalyst.org/knowledge/women-ceos-sp-500.

Wooley, Anita and Thomas Malone. "Defend Your Research: What Makes a Team Smarter? More Women." *Harvard Business Review,* June 2011. http://hbr.org/2011/06/defend-your-research-what-makes-a-team-smarter-more-women/ar/1.

NOTES

Introduction: Why This Book Is Different

1. Tom Rath and Barry Conchie, *Strengths Based Leadership: Great Leaders, Teams, and Why People Follow* (New York: Gallup Press, 2008), 1.

2. Benjamin Snyder, "Half of Us Have Quit Our Job because of a Bad Boss," *Fortune*, April 2, 2015, http://fortune.com/2015/04/02/quit-reasons/http://fortune.com/2015/04/02/quit-reasons/.

Chapter 2: Knowing Yourself

3. Susan Sorenson and Keri Garman, "How to Tackle U.S. Employees' Stagnating Employee Engagement," *Gallup Business Journal*, June 11, 2013, http://www.gallup.com/businessjournal/162953/tackle-employees-stagnating-engagement.aspx.

4. Michael Bungay Stanier, *Do More Great Work: Stop the Busywork. Start the Work That Matters* (New York: Workman Publishing Company, Inc., 2010), 33.

5. Rath and Conchie, *Strengths Based Leadership*, 2.

6. Michael Bungay Stanier, *Do More Great Work*, 33.

7. John Hall, "10 Ways to Help Others That Will Lead You to Success," *Fortune*, May 26, 2013, http://www.forbes.com/sites/johnhall/2013/05/26/10-ways-to-help-others-that-will-lead-you-to-success/#481b3e471e4f.

8. Christine McLaren, "Knowing Yourself First, Part I," *Monday Mentor*, June 25, 2012, https://mondaymentor.wordpress.com/2012/06/25/knowing-yourself-first-part-i/.

Chapter 3: Knowing Others

9. "Corporate Culture," *Inc. Magazine*, February 8, 2017, http://www.inc.com/encyclopedia/corporate-culture.html.

10. Fred Laluyaux, "Perception vs. Reality: Do You Know What Your Real Company Culture Is?" *Inc. Magazine*, October 13, 2014, http://www.inc.com/fred-laluyaux/perception-vs-reality-do-you-know-what-your-real-company-culture-is.html.

11. Jeff Thompson, PhD, "Is Nonverbal Communications a Numbers Game?" *Psychology Today*, September 30, 2011, https://www.psychologytoday.com/blog/beyond-words/201109/is-nonverbal-communication-numbers-game.

12. John M. Gottman, PhD, *The Seven Principles for Making Marriage Work: A Practical Guide from the Country's Foremost Relationship Expert* (New York: Three Rivers Press, 1999), 29.

Chapter 4: Leadership Fundamentals and Authority

13. Rath and Conchie, *Strengths Based Leadership*, 2–3.

14. "9 Things Employees Want from Their Managers (and 5 Things They Don't)," *HR Specialist*, February 6, 2017, http://www. thehrspecialist.com/article.aspx?articleid=32033&cigx=d. nac, stid.2942, sid.115314, lid.11, mid.1708.

15. Ronald E. Riggio, Ira Chaleff, and Jean Lipman-Blumen, *The Art of Followership: How Great Followers Create Great Leaders and Organizations* (San Francisco: Jossey-Bass, 2008), 121.

16. Ibid.

17. Ronald A. Heifetz, *Leadership without Easy Answers* (Cambridge, MA: The Belknap Press of Harvard University Press, 1997), 102.

18. Paul Hersey, Kenneth H. Blanchard, and Dewey E. Johnson, *Management of Organizational Behavior: Leading Human Resources* (Upper Saddle River, NJ: Prentice Hall, Inc., 2001), 211.

19. Hersey, Blanchard, and Johnson, *Management of Organizational Behavior*, 211.

20. Ibid., 210.

21. Ibid., 212.

22. Ibid., 212.

23. Ibid., 210.

24. Ibid., 212.

Chapter 5: Engaging and Retaining Others

25. Kevin Kruse, "What is Employee Engagement?" *Forbes*, June 22, 2012, http://www.forbes.com/sites/kevinkruse/2012/06/22/employee-engagement-what-and-why/#243c43a84629.

26. Ibid.

Chapter 6: Coaching Others

27. Kris Duggan, "Why the Annual Performance Review is Going Extinct," *Fast Company*, October 20, 2015, https://www.fastcompany.com/3052135/the-future-of-work/why-the-annual-performance-review-is-going-extinct.

Chapter 7: Emotional Intelligence

28. Daniel Goleman, *Working with Emotional Intelligence* (New York: Bantam Books, 1998), 3.

29. Ibid., 26–27.

30. Daniel Goleman, "What Makes a Leader?" *Harvard Business Review*, January 2004, 3.

31. Ibid., 3.

32. Ibid., 3.

33. Catherine Chen, "Effective Leadership: How Not to Take Things Personally," *Huffington Post*, November 7, 2013, http://www.huffingtonpost.com/catherine-chen-phd/effective-leadership-how-_b_4226286.html.

34. Goleman, "What Makes a Leader?" 6.

35. Ibid., 8–9.

36. Goleman, *Working with Emotional Intelligence*, 10.

37. Goleman, "What Makes a Leader?" 8.

38. Goleman, *Working with Emotional Intelligence*, 33–34.

Chapter 8: Influencing Others

39. Tom Peters, "The Brand Called You," *Fast Company*, August 31, 1997, https://www.fastcompany.com/28905/brand-called-you.

40. Norm Smallwood, "Define Your Personal Leadership Brand in Five Steps," *Harvard Business Review*, March 29, 2010, https://hbr.org/2010/03/define-your-personal-leadership.

Chapter 9: A How-To: The Five Most Common Career Changes

41. "Career Change Statistics: You Will Change Careers 7 Times in Your Life?" Careers Advice Online, accessed February 5, 2017, http://www.careers-advice-online.com/career-change-statistics.html.

42. Ibid.

43. Ibid.

44. John B. Horrigan, "Lifelong Learning and Technology," Pew Research Center, March 22, 2016, http://www.pewinternet.org/2016/03/22/lifelong-learning-and-technology/.

45. Anthonia Akitunde, "Back to School: What You Must Think about before Furthering Your Education after 50," *Huffington Post*, August 17, 2012, http://www.huffington-post.com/2012/08/17/back-to-school-adult-education-stu-dent-loans_n_1773801.html.

46. Jolynn Shoemaker, Amy Brown, and Rachel Barbour, "A Revolutionary Change: Making the Workplace More Flexible," *Solutions Journal* 2 (2011): 52–62, http://www.thesolutionsjournal.com/node/889.

47. Ibid.

Chapter 10: Senior Leadership

48. Heifetz, *Leadership without Easy Answers*, 22.

49. Ibid., 126.

50. Ibid., 138–139.

51. Ibid., 139–141.

52. Ibid., 141–142.

53. Ibid., 142–144.

54. Ibid., 144.

55. Ibid., 276.

Chapter 11: Leading Global Teams

56. Charlene M. Solomon and Michael S. Schell, *Managing across Cultures: The Seven Keys to Doing Business with a Global Mindset* (New York: McGraw Hill, 2009), 52.

57. Ibid., 77.

58. Ibid., 77–80.

59. Ibid., 82–94.

60. Ibid., 95.

61. Ibid., 98–99.

62. Ibid., 102–105.

63. Ibid., 117–119.

64. Ibid., 142–145.

65. Ibid., 167–170.

66. Ibid., 188–190.

67. Ibid., 205–207.

Chapter 12: Progress (and the Lack Thereof) for Women and Minorities

68. Anita Wooley and Thomas Malone, "Defend Your Research: What Makes a Team Smarter? More Women," *Harvard Business Review*, June 2011, http://hbr.org/2011/06/defend-your-research-what-makes-a-team-smarter-more-women/ar/1.

69. Natalie Burg, "Businesses Harness the Power of Diversity for Growth," *Forbes*, December 24, 2013, http://www.forbes.com/sites/capitalonespark/2013/12/24/businesses-harness-the-power-of-diversity-for-growth/#2021f25bcc15.

70. Ibid.

71. Alison Kenney Paul, Thom McElroy, and Tonie Leatherberry, "Diversity as an Engine of Innovation," Deloitte University Press, January 1, 2011, http://dupress.com/wp-content/uploads/2011/01/US_deloittereview_Diversity_as_an_Engine_of_Innovation_Jan11.pdf.

72. Amelia Costigan, "5 Facts You Need to Know about Buying Power," *Catalyst*, May 20, 2015, http://www.catalyst.org/zing/5-facts-you-need-know-about-buying-power.

73. Lauren Tara LaCapra, "Morgan Stanley CEO Says Companies Need More Female Executives," *Reuters*, April 2, 2014, http://www.reuters.com/article/2014/04/03/morganstanley-porat-idUSL1N0MV03N20140403.

74. Rod Robinson, "Four Diversity Supplier Reporting Trends," *Wharton Magazine*, May 14, 2005, http://whartonmagazine.com/blogs/four-supplier-diversity-reporting-trends/.

75. Gillian White, "Women Are Owning More and More Small Businesses," *The Atlantic*, April 17, 2015, http://www.theatlantic.com/business/archive/2015/04/women-are-owning-more-and-more-small-businesses/390642/.

76. White, Ibid.

77. "Los Angeles County a Microcosm of Nation's Diverse Collection of Business Owners, Census Bureau Reports," US Bureau of the Census, December 15, 2015, http://www.census.gov/newsroom/press-releases/2015/cb15-209.html.

78. "Women on Corporate Boards Globally," *Catalyst*, January 4, 2017, http://www.catalyst.org/knowledge/women-corporate-boards-globally.

79. "Women CEOs of the S&P 500," *Catalyst*, January 3, 2017, http://www.catalyst.org/knowledge/women-ceos-sp-500.

80. Judith Warner, "The Women's Leadership Gap: Women's Leadership by the Numbers," Center for American Progress, August 4, 2015, https://www.american-progress.org/issues/women/report/2015/08/04/118743/the-womens-leadership-gap/.

81. Jenna Goudreau, "Why Do Women Round Down while Men Round Up?" *Forbes*, January 11, 2012, http://www.forbes.com/sites/jennagoudreau/2012/01/11/women-round-down-confidence-career-advancement/#407bf50423e9.

82. Horace McCormick, "The Real Effects of Unconscious Bias in the Workplace," UNC Kenan-Flagler Business School (2015): 5, http://www.kenan-flagler.unc.edu/~/media/Files/documents/executive-development/unc-white-paper-the-real-effects-of-unconscious-bias-in-the-workplace-Final.

83. Ibid., 3.

84. Ibid., 6.

Chapter 13: Bringing It All Together

85. Michael M. Lombardo and Robert W. Eichinger, *Career Architect Development Planner*, 4th ed., (Minneapolis, MN: Lominger International, 2007), v.

86. Edwin A. Locke, "Motivation through Conscious Goal Setting," *Applied & Preventative Psychology*, 5 (1996): 119–120, https://www.researchgate.net/profile/Edwin_Locke/publication/222720003_Motivation_through_Conscious_Goal_Setting/links/00b4952d42aa12d430000000.pdf.

87. George T. Doran, "There's a S.M.A.R.T. Way to Write Management's Goals and Objectives," *Management Review*, Vol. 70, Issue 11 (1981), 35–36.

88. Leigh Stringer, "The Essential Ingredient You're Missing in Achieving Your Goals," *Huffington Post*, June 9, 2016, http://www.huffingtonpost.com/entry/the-essential-ingredient-youre-missing-in-achieving-your-goals_us_5730ecc3e4b016f37896af06.

www.ingramcontent.com/pod-product-compliance
Lightning Source LLC
Chambersburg PA
CBHW071539200326
41519CB00021BB/6538